If we **go in** here, we're **dead** aren't we?

That's the **coolest** thing I've ever seen!

It's not a **kit car**, it's a **Lamborghini**, you philistine!

BBC Children's Books
Published by the Penguin Group
Penguin Books Ltd, 80 Strand, London, WC2R 0RL, England
Penguin Group (Australia) Ltd, 250 Camberwell Road,
Camberwell, Victoria 3124, Australia (a division of Pearson
Australia Group Pty Ltd)
Canada, India, New Zealand, South Africa

Published by BBC Children's Books, 2008
Text and design © Children's Character Books, 2008

10 9 8 7 6 5 4 3 2 1

Pages 8-9, 14-15, 28-29, 38-42, 50-51, 70-82 written by David Carr
Pages 6-7, 10-11, 16-17, 30-31, 34-37, 44-47, 60-63, 66-67, 84-90
written by Jonathan Empson
Pages 12-13, 22-25, 28-29, 32-33, 43, 48-49, 64-65 written
by Mark Hillsdon
Pages 18-21, 52-59 written by Jason Loborik
Pages 68-69, 86-89 written by Dan Newman

Designed by Dan Green

ISBN: 978-1-40590-455-1

Printed in Europe

Gear

The Official Annual 2009

Contents

Meet the Team

A huge crew of people including producers, directors, researchers, mechanics, drivers and hair stylists slave for months to prepare every Top Gear episode. No one sees this intensive preparation though, you just get to see three blokes and The Stig driving cars. And occasionally blowing them up, driving them through deserts, playing ice hockey, or launching them into space. Looks like fun, doesn't it?

JEREMY CLARKSON
a.k.a. Jezza

> **Power!**

Born: Jeremy Charles Robert Clarkson, Doncaster, 1960.

Drives: Lamborghini Gallardo Spyder, Mercedes-Benz SLK55 AMG, Volvo XC90, Toyota Land Cruiser, Ford Focus, ex-military Land Rover Defender.

Jeremy loves to drive. He once drove a Bugatti Veyron at 240mph in Europe. He also once drove a Rolls-Royce into a swimming pool. And even more bizarrely, he drove a Toybota across the Channel. However, the most important thing to remember is that Jeremy has strong opinions and is never, ever wrong.

JAMES MAY
a.k.a. Captain Slow

Born: James Daniel May, Bristol, 1963.

Drives: Bentley, Porsche Boxster, Porsche 911, Fiat Panda, Jaguar.

James really loves cars, but rarely drives them in the right direction, or at any great speed. James also likes to know how machines work and enjoys explaining these facts in detail to Jeremy and Richard. They really love it, too.

> I am actually the only **proper bloke** on this programme.

RICHARD HAMMOND
a.k.a. The Hamster

THE STIG
a.k.a. The Stig

> I am a driving **God!**

Born: Richard Mark Hammond, Birmingham, 1969.

Drives: Porsche 911 (x2), Dodge Charger, Land Rover (x2), Morgan V6 Roadster, 1968 Ford Mustang, various kit cars.

If ever a car needs to be frozen, drowned or struck by lightning, Richard's the man who'll sit inside while it happens. He also becomes quite attached to cars. Remember Oliver?

Born: Or perhaps created. May have been raised by wolves.

Drives: Fast.

The following may or may not be true about His Royal Stigness: his earwax tastes like Turkish delight; there's an airport in Russia named after him; he appears on high-value stamps in Sweden; his tears are adhesive; he has two sets of knees; he urinates high-octane petrol.

7

The Stig Files

There are many rumours about The Stig. Some of them fact, quite a few fiction. But who has the answers? Who can be believed?

Jeremy, Richard and James aren't talking and you can bet The Stig won't spill. So all we can rely upon is what we already know.
Let the facts speak for themselves...

He is **wanted** by the **CIA**

Name: The Stig a.k.a. The White Stig, His Stigness, Grand Earl of Stigwich etc etc.

D.O.B (Date of Being): 2 November, 2003. Some say he was born in space and arrived on Earth the day Black Stig (rumoured to be his father) drove off the HMS Invincible. This information remains unconfirmed.

Place of being: The Stig operates out of the Top Gear studios in Surrey, where he keeps a small, but tastefully-furnished bungalow. Some say he also has a studio apartment at the top of the London Eye.

Interests other than driving: Driving.

Languages: The Stig has turned his hand to Italian, Spanish and numerous other languages, learned primarily while doing Power Laps.

Career highlights: The Ascari A10 (fastest power lap ever), fastest lap time in a 'reasonably priced Suzuki Liana', refusing to answer a mobile phone.

Career low points: Being arrested in a Caterham Seven kit car, running the Koenigsegg CCX into a tyre wall, having to catch public transport.

His **earwax** tastes like **Turkish delight**

His **skin** has the texture of **dolphins**

He can **melt concrete** on contact

His favourite food is **raw meat**

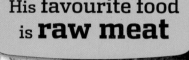

He has a **digital** face

Interest-Stig Quiz

Test your knowledge of the Grand Earl of Stigwich and his many motoring exploits.

01 What did The Stig drive down the ski-jump at Lillehammer, the site of the 1994 Winter Olympics?

02 It's the only car The Stig has ever spun off the Top Gear test track.

03 Apart from really bad music, name three other things The Stig listens to while completing his Power Laps.

04 Complete the following: Some say he appears on high-value stamps in...

05 What time did The Stig do in the Ascari A10; his fastest lap time to date?

Top Gear Test Track

I t was designed by Lotus, but unlike most Lotuses, it's nearly two miles long. Yes, it's Top Gear's test track, based at a top-secret location (Dunsford Park, Surrey, just off the A281).

03 Hammerhead

The Follow-through

04

05

Chicago Corner

02

Bentley Bend

06

Bacharach Bend

07

03
Hammerhead
A left-right into this tricky and tight corner, so named because it's shaped like... um... some sort of tool... wait, it'll come to me...

02
Chicago Corner
Billie Piper managed to get lost at this right-hander, but didn't actually end up in Chicago.

05
The Follow-through
The fastest part of the circuit, where drivers can experience the bowel-loosening terror of a reasonably-priced car going flat-out.

04
Willson Bend
The only place where The Stig has crashed. As we all know, he was driving the Koenigsegg CCX. It's a fast right-hander (just don't go too fast).

01
Crooner Curve
The first corner after the start, a fast left-hander, so-called because drivers wail, 'Oooooooooo!' Singer Lionel Ritchie certainly did when he lost a wheel taking on this corner.

SKREEEEEEEEEE

Crooner Curve

01

09

Gambon Corner

08

09
The Finish Line!

08
Gambon Corner
Named after actor Sir Michael Gambon, who managed to get the Reasonably Priced Car up on two wheels while going round it.

07
Bacharach Bend
'I Say a Little Prayer' is a song by Burt Bacharach, and celebs are praying they'll last the distance at this point. Didn't work for actor David Soul, who broke his gearbox here. Twice.

06
Bentley Bend
A fast left-hander. Crashing here simply wouldn't do, old chap.

EEEEEYOOWWWW

Which Presenter are You?

Answer these questions to find out. Simply tally up how many answers of each colour you have. For example, if your answers are mostly blue splats you are most like Jeremy, if you have more orange splats you're like Richard, etc etc.

Do you have a sneaky love of motorbikes?
Yes   No

Do you enjoy over-using words like 'biblical', 'awesome' and 'utterly'?
Yes   No

Have you ever driven a car around the BBC?
Yes   No

Do you prefer life in the slow lane?
Yes   No

Have you ever sunk a car in the English Channel?
Yes   No

Do you loathe caravanning holidays?
Yes   No

Are you good at map reading?
Yes   No

Do you own the world's largest collection of love ballad CDs?
Yes   No

Can your voice only be heard by cats?
Yes   No

Do you think driving a car full of water is good clean fun or downright dumb?
Dumb   Fun

You're most like... Jeremy

You love cars and everything to do with them – especially fast, red, Italian ones. You always say what you think and always believe you are right. For example, your Toybota sank but you still believe you won the Amphibious Car Challenge.

.... blue splats

You're most like... Richard

You're a bit of a daredevil and enjoy a challenge – the more ridiculous the better. You've a mixed taste in cars and can get as excited about a good, solid 4x4 as you can by a sleek Lamborghini or powerful Porsche.

.... orange splats

Given the choice, would you make the game of cricket illegal? Yes / No

Does knowing how an engine works get you excited? Yes / No

Do you need a haircut? Yes / No

Do you use teeth whitener? Yes / No

Have you ever launched a Reliant Robin into the side of a hill? Yes / No

Do you sleep upside down like a bat? Yes / No

Is you favourite car a Land Rover? Yes / No

Do you own more than three pairs of faded jeans? Yes / No

Would you eat a tortoise? Yes / No

Are you actually quite good at playing the guitar? Yes / No

Have badgers ever lived in your hair? Yes / No

Have you ever raced a man on roller skates in an Aston Martin? Yes / No

Did you invent Branston Pickle? Yes / No

Have you ever eaten spam at the North Pole? Yes / No

Are you nicknamed after a small rodent? Yes / No

You're most like... James

You're passionate about cars but not just because they're speed machines. To you, a car is a real thing of beauty, something to be cherished and looked after, not thrashed round a track in a cloud of smoke.

You're most like... The Stig

You're the strong silent type who likes to play your cards close to your chest. And drive very fast cars. You live for speed and the type of music that not even your Dad would listen to.

!!!.......... **brown splats**

/............ **white splats**

13

Hidden Star

Fill in the answers to the questions in the grid below, then drive the car straight down the middle to spell out the name of a recent Star in a Reasonably Priced Car!

1 Make and model of the current Reasonably Priced Car.
2 Nickname of Richard's attempt at an amphibious vehicle.
3 Country where Koenigseggs are built.
4 Car launched down a ski-jump during the Top Gear Winter Olympics.
5 Racetrack where the Top Gear presenters took part in a 24-hour diesel endurance race.
6 The Stig's preferred clothing colour.
7 Maker of the indestructible pick-up.
8 Name of the last corner on the Top Gear test track.
9 James May's middle name.
10 Animal symbol of Lamborghini.
11 Car that Jeremy used to carry a truffle across Europe.
12 Name of Richard's African Opel Kadett.
13 Maker of the Zonda supercar.

Spot the Difference

Though they were supposed to be out road-testing three stylish offerings from Audi, Mazda and Alfa Romeo, the lads decided to cast good fashion sense aside and prance around a Scottish golf course dressed like, well, golfers!

See if you can spot the 12 differences between the images below.

Which Supercar Suits You?

Pick a car, any car... So you've been saving your pocket money all year (and your allowance is about £10,000 a week). You decide to buy yourself a supercar. But which one? Yes, all these cars go fast, but they're all different. Follow our flowchart to help you decide.

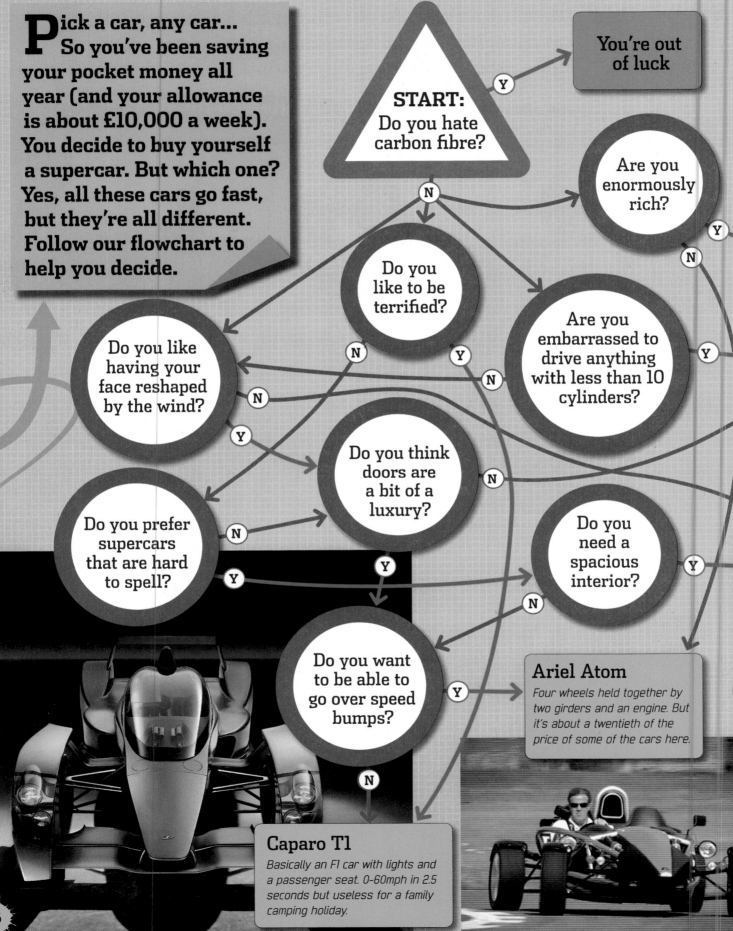

START: Do you hate carbon fibre?

You're out of luck

Are you enormously rich?

Do you like to be terrified?

Are you embarrassed to drive anything with less than 10 cylinders?

Do you like having your face reshaped by the wind?

Do you think doors are a bit of a luxury?

Do you prefer supercars that are hard to spell?

Do you need a spacious interior?

Do you want to be able to go over speed bumps?

Ariel Atom
Four wheels held together by two girders and an engine. But it's about a twentieth of the price of some of the cars here.

Caparo T1
Basically an F1 car with lights and a passenger seat. 0-60mph in 2.5 seconds but useless for a family camping holiday.

16

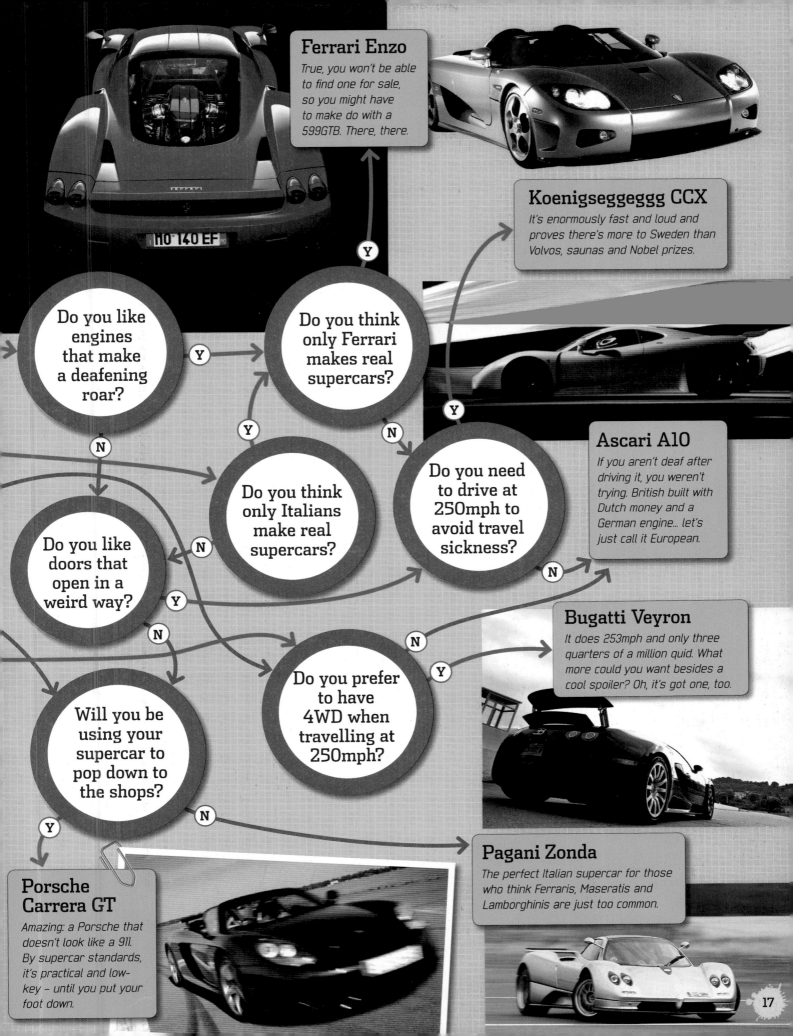

Ferrari Enzo

True, you won't be able to find one for sale, so you might have to make do with a 599GTB. There, there.

Koenigseggeggg CCX

It's enormously fast and loud and proves there's more to Sweden than Volvos, saunas and Nobel prizes.

Do you like engines that make a deafening roar?

Do you think only Ferrari makes real supercars?

Ascari A10

If you aren't deaf after driving it, you weren't trying. British built with Dutch money and a German engine... let's just call it European.

Do you like doors that open in a weird way?

Do you think only Italians make real supercars?

Do you need to drive at 250mph to avoid travel sickness?

Bugatti Veyron

It does 253mph and only three quarters of a million quid. What more could you want besides a cool spoiler? Oh, it's got one, too.

Will you be using your supercar to pop down to the shops?

Do you prefer to have 4WD when travelling at 250mph?

Porsche Carrera GT

Amazing: a Porsche that doesn't look like a 911. By supercar standards, it's practical and low-key – until you put your foot down.

Pagani Zonda

The perfect Italian supercar for those who think Ferraris, Maseratis and Lamborghinis are just too common.

Y N

Cool Wheels Word Search

There are some pretty cool cars in the list below, but can you find them all in the grid? Words can go up, down, forwards, backwards or diagonally.

I think **Koenigsegg** is Swedish for, 'Oh no, my head's just **exploded**!'

```
O E U S A I O O O U D N M R G T A N
X A P R V C A U D R A T E R C D N E
O E T E B A T O T C P M Y P L A I D
A O E V S V A P D S O T I I B A A O
E G A T N A V N I T R A M N O T S A
A G S C D K A X H Y S A A I A N T D
L O A A T A T C S A C O A X K I O N
G O N M O A O C S S H T A G U I N O
F Y T F N Z R G A A E H E D E G M Z
A A M U O R N G B I C C N S S A A I
O I T R S R F E X A A E I G E X R N
O F A J N E D S I E Y R T G T G T A
A X S E N O X G A R M O M N N E I G
S N O R Y E V I T T A G U B M E N A
A T N E T N N N G T N R A C C R D P
A M N I N N E E S E A T R T R G B H
E N E R S F O O G N M X C E H Z S G
J A G U A R X K R N R I A H F T N X
```

LOTUS EXIGE

ASTON MARTIN VANTAGE

PORSCHE CAYMAN

JAGUAR XKR

PAGANI ZONDA

BUGATTI VEYRON

ASTON MARTIN DBS

FERRARI ENZO

KOENIGSEGG CCX

FORD GT

Name That Badge

Reckon you know your car badges? We've got rid of the names of the ones below and now you've got to work out which car maker goes with which symbol. The jumbled-up words alongside might help, or may just confuse things more!

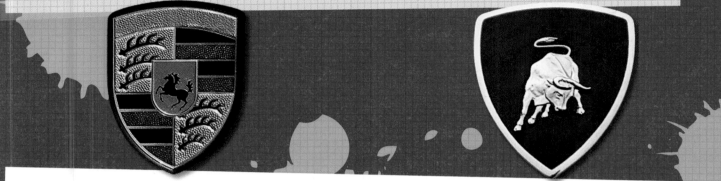

1. SO PERCH

_____

2. LOG HIM BRIAN

_____

3. RARE FIR

_____

4. SWANK GLOVE

_____

5. SUTOL

_____

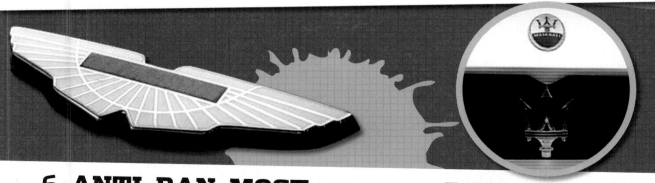

6. ANTI RAN MOST

_____

7. ITS MA EAR

_____

Caravan Holiday!

Jeremy, James and Richard have decided to find out what all the fuss is about with caravan holidays. After all, 850,000 people can't be wrong, can they? There must be some reason they decide to clog up the roads all summer...

How to play:

Choose whether to play as Jeremy, Richard, James or Top Gear Dog. Use coins as counters and place them on the start. The shortest player goes first. Roll a die to make your way along the road to the end of the holiday, following instructions on any squares you land on.

START
You decide to go on a caravan holiday. Lose all credibility, but go ahead anyway. *Roll a 1 to start.*

Hook up your van at the second attempt, and struggle to fit the extended mirrors. *Miss a turn.*

Head off for Devon at top speed: 30mph. *Only move if you roll 1, 2 or 3 until you reach the site.*

Miss a turn while you stop for lunch: Pork pie and scotch eggs. Remember to put everything away properly.

You've done 52 miles in three and a quarter hours. *Roll again to try and speed up.*

Captain Slow at the wheel of a Kia towing a caravan.

Secretly, he is delighted.

You start arguing about which way to go. *For your next turn, move back 1 space.*

What the hell?

That's... bad.

Miss another turn when you hit a post leaving the garage.

Top Gear Dog has been sick. Stop to clean him up. *Miss a turn.*

I can't bear the **shame!**

There's a hundred cars behind you. *Miss a turn to pull over and hide.*

1 2 3 4 5 6 7 8 9 10 11 12 13 14 15 16 17 18 19 20 21 22 23

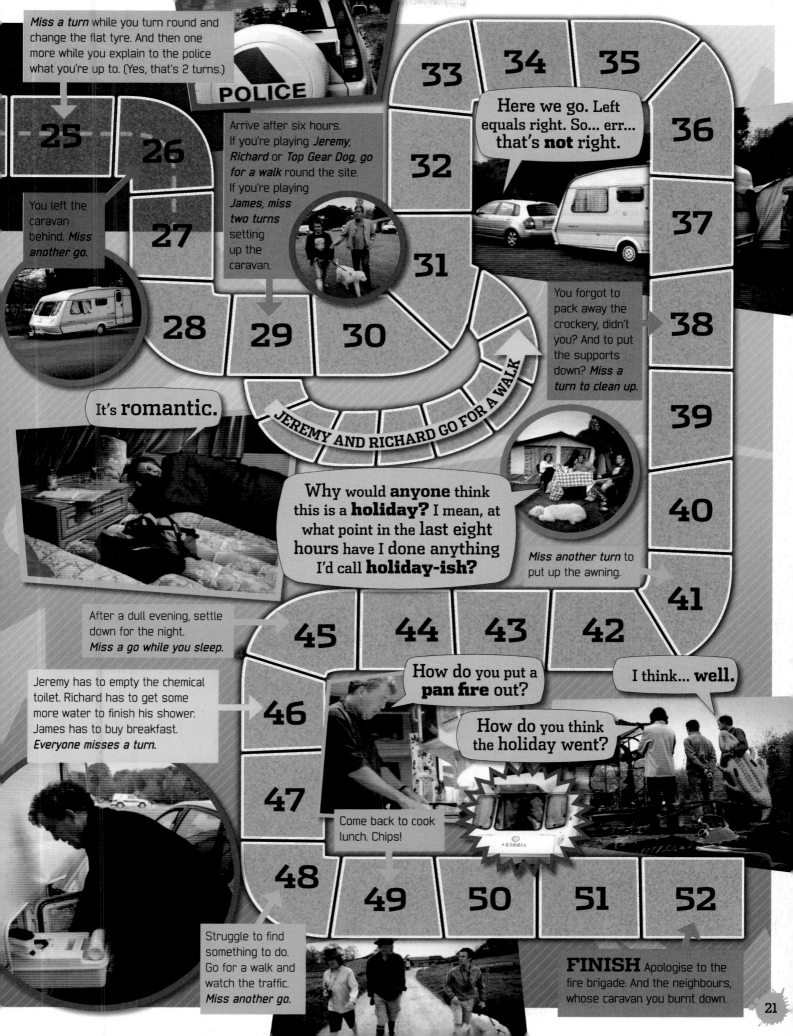

Miss a turn while you turn round and change the flat tyre. And then one more while you explain to the police what you're up to. (Yes, that's 2 turns.)

POLICE

25

26

You left the caravan behind. *Miss another go.*

27

Arrive after six hours. If you're playing *Jeremy*, *Richard* or *Top Gear Dog*, go *for a walk* round the site. If you're playing *James*, miss *two turns* setting up the caravan.

28

29

30

31

32

33

34

35

Here we go. Left equals right. So... err... that's **not** right.

36

37

You forgot to pack away the crockery, didn't you? And to put the supports down? *Miss a turn to clean up.*

38

39

40

Miss another turn to put up the awning.

41

JEREMY AND RICHARD GO FOR A WALK

It's **romantic.**

Why would **anyone** think this is a **holiday?** I mean, at what point in the last eight hours have I done anything I'd call **holiday-ish?**

After a dull evening, settle down for the night. *Miss a go while you sleep.*

45

44

43

42

I think... **well.**

Jeremy has to empty the chemical toilet. Richard has to get some more water to finish his shower. James has to buy breakfast. *Everyone misses a turn.*

46

How do you put a **pan fire** out?

How do you think the holiday went?

47

Come back to cook lunch. Chips!

Elddis

48

Struggle to find something to do. Go for a walk and watch the traffic. *Miss another go.*

49

50

51

52

FINISH Apologise to the fire brigade. And the neighbours, whose caravan you burnt down.

Polar Challenge –
The Fools of the Wild

We're here because we're gonna have a **race. Four hundred miles** over mostly **frozen ocean** in that direction to the **North Pole.**

Magnetic North Pole

SPAM

A tin of Spam

Snow drifts

A crashed plane

A dead seal

Ice boulders

Polar bear

Very thin ice

Slushy ice

Thin Ice

Ice

Resolute – the most Northerly town in Canada

Team Truck involves Jeremy, James and a jazzed-up Toyota Hilux.

Specialist engineers from Iceland had got their welding gear out and made a few key alterations to the truck.

No one had **ever** tried to drive to the North Pole. **Wonder why?**

I think we're all gonna **die.**

There's new heavy-duty suspension.

The tyres are handmade and cost £2,500 each.

And there's a special guard around the sump to protect it from the ice.

The wheels are massive to give extra height and help them through the snow.

Team Dog involves novice skier Richard, Mattie McNair, one of the world's leading sledge dog explorers, and ten snarling, snapping huskies.

Richard hangs on here.

The dogs pull here.

He's a **plucky Brit** and like all plucky Brits he's going to **come in second.**

Um, that's about it.

Roll in the **snow,** Jeremy!

On the way they would encounter ice boulders as big as cathedrals, polar bears the size of hatchbacks and temperatures that would freeze the fuel in the tanks.

To toughen the lads up, they were sent on an Arctic training course. But they weren't really taking things seriously until they saw what frostbite could do to certain parts of the body.

The trio's attempt to put a tent up seriously annoyed the SAS trainer. But he got his revenge by pushing Jeremy into a freezing Arctic ice hole as part of his survival training. In the end, polar explorer legend Sir Ranulph Fiennes was drafted in to drum into them that the Arctic is an extremely dangerous place. After all, he'd lost several fingers to frostbite, so he should know.

Having a poo was a major topic of discussion. So Jeremy decided to attach a toilet seat to the rear of the truck. He called it his bumper dumper.

And while someone sat on 'the throne' the other stood guard with a shotgun, in case any polar bears got a whiff of what was going on.

You will all start hating each other because of the extreme cold... The hatred is very **real** and you don't want to **laugh** about it.

Oh God. Sorry, sorry, sorry, sorry, sorry, sorry, **sorry.**

They also learnt the theory behind doing a poo when it's -50°C outside. Do it quickly!

Richard proved hopeless at skiing.

Clarkson, I know it's you, you **insufferable oaf.** I'm on the BEEP throne.

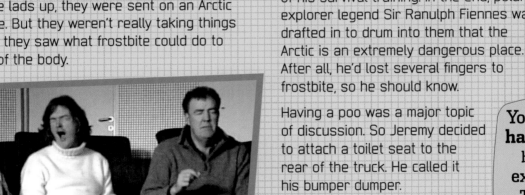

VRROOOMM

23

> This is **brilliant!**

> **First time** at the wheel, James has **managed** to put it basically into the **sea.**

Thing weren't going well for Richard who was over 50 miles behind. To try and make up time they began travelling at night. And that just made Richard more tired, more irritable and, let's face, a little bit more mad.

James and Jeremy, meanwhile, were starting to get cocky and discussing how they'd celebrate their victory. In a strange moment, James said he was going to eat a tin of Spam as soon as he got there.

But gradually the ice started to get really thin. So thin that it turned blue because you could see the water through it, sloshing around just a few centimetres below. And thin, slushy ice meant a stuck truck.

> This is **BEEP** **scary.**

> How on **Earth** did nature come up with **that?**

> We're facing a **problem.** There **is** no other **way** through here.

> It's **very** hard work and **very** cold and quite lonely **out there.**

It suddenly dawned on Jeremy and James that they were quite literally skating on thin ice… in a three tonne truck… 1,500 miles away from the nearest hospital.

Finally, they were clear of the thin ice. But they soon had a new problem: massive ice boulders blocking the route. The truck couldn't drive over the jagged ice or through the snowdrifts in between them. The only option left for the dynamic duo was to get out a chainsaw and cut their way through. Progress was slow.

This was Richard's chance to claw back some of the 90 miles he was behind. So Mattie unveiled her secret weapon – a kite!

With Mattie on skis being towed by a kite, the sledge was much lighter and the dogs were more motivated as they tried to keep up with the 'pack leader'.

Frustrated at being stuck in an icy wilderness for two days, Jeremy lost the plot! And he took it out on the Hilux, crashing over some thick ice and puncturing the spare fuel tank. Oh dear. Now running out of fuel was a very real issue.

Yeah, now we're making progress!

Imagine surviving that **plane crash** and then finding yourself **here.**

This **incredible** machine had **breached** what the experts had said would be an **impregnable** wall. It had taken on the impossible and **it had won.**

BA-DOOOM

Meanwhile, Richard had made good time over the frozen boulder field to edge his sledge into the lead.

It had taken three days of almost non-stop driving but the truck also made it through the boulders.

And slowly the truck began to reel in the dog team, as they sped across the frozen wilderness.

But with the pole a tantalising ten miles away, the truck came up against another wall of snow and ice. Finally they crawled out the other side. But were they in the lead?

It's flat, it's so **smooth** and no more going up and down!

All they had to do now was match their position with the coordinates for the pole on their Satnav…

Current position
t.   :N 78° 35' 7
ng. :W 104° 11' 9

You've **done** it?

I'd set out to **prove** that polar exploration could be **easy.** But, it **isn't.** It's **brutal** and **savage.**

Hammond?

Yes?

We're at the **North Pole!**

We've done it! **We're here!**

Mashed-up Marques

Here are some fiendishly difficult anagrams for you to work out. In fact, they're so hard, we've decided to help you a bit by giving you a list of possible answers.

We say a bit of help because we've also thrown in a couple of red herrings too, just to keep things interesting.

1. Races Rear Porch _____

2. I rough a limo cab gremlin _____

3. A male riot _____

4. A Fandango Zip _____

5. Bad wet ill crow _____

6. Maria Boaster _____

7. Darling oaf _____

8. A Scram In Sin _____

9. Cereal Peanuts _____

10. Vegan error _____

Here are your choices:

Pagani Zonda F
Lamborghini Murcielago
Ford Focus
Renault Espace
Maserati Bora
Porsche Carrera
Vauxhall Vectra

Ariel Atom
Bowler Wildcat
Fiat Panda
Ford Anglia
Morris Oxford
Range Rover
Nissan Micra

A Hidden Gem

Some say that quizzes in annuals are too easy. We don't agree as we've made this quiz really hard. Or as Jeremy might say, it's a quiz of biblical proportions.

Here's what you have to do. Solve the clues and write your answers in the grid. Now rearrange the letters in the shaded boxes to spell out the name of something we just love featuring on the show.

Oh, one last thing before you start. The clues aren't actually in the right order. Just thought you'd like to know.

Ok then, off you go...

FWAP

8. Pet nickname for Richard.

1. This was the make of our famous Indestructible Pick-up Truck.

6. Lewis ... who? So nearly a champion first time round.

2. Captain Slow took this beast up to 253mph.

10. 'Great' British company that used to make classics like the Princess.

3. Top English racing circuit.

5. The game played by ten Suzuki Swifts during the Winter Olympics Special.

7. Jeremy loved this supercar so much, he bought one.

9. This marque has a fighting bull for its logo.

4. Famous for their 911.

Now rearrange the letters in the shaded boxes to spell...

Some say he's more machine than man, and that the outline of his left nipple is exactly the same shape as the Nürburgring. He is The Stig – the world's greatest tame racing driver.

But who exactly is The Stig? How did The Stig become The Stig? And is it possible to be as good a test driver as The Stig?

However, for those still suffering delusions of grandeur, here are five semi-useful tips that will soon have you basking in the high-octane afterglow of The Stig.

He **sleeps** upside down **like a bat**

01. Choose a suit

Obviously white has already been taken and black is currently lying somewhere at the bottom of the North Atlantic, so you'll need another colour that's:

a. Cool (because The Stig is);

b. Eye-catching (because you're going to be moving stupidly fast); and

c. Easy to get stains out of (we'll let you work that one out).

02. Learn something about cars

The only way to tame the beast is to know the beast. Read up on the mechanics of cars, not just the interiors. Get to know the engines, power to weight ratios, handling, performance, transmissions and aerodynamics of the world's fastest vehicles. Because an in-car DVD player is not going to do you much good while you're taking a corner in a Pagani Zonda.

His **teeth glow** in the **dark**

03. Learn something about the track

Aside from the car and the driver, the other crucial element in a successful test drive is the track. Knowing the circuit is the sign of a good test driver. Missing a corner and ending up slamming into a tyre wall is usually the sign of a bad one.

He can **smell** corners

04. Choose your in-car entertainment

The Stig amuses himself by listening to language courses and country and western music and easy-listening. So find the tunes that spur on the speed and stick to them!

05. Have no fear

Or, at least, show no fear. This means not saying anything to anyone. People will either think you're utterly fearless or that you have no tongue.

FACT!

Described by Jeremy as 'the longest and most terrifying race track in the world', the Nürburgring in Germany is 13 miles long and has 73 corners (the Top Gear test track has 8). As such, it is seen by car-makers around the world as the perfect place to test prototypes of their new vehicles.

the Nürburgring

Sabine Schmitz

Top 10 Supercars

So here they are: the best supercars ever to fall into Top Gear's sweaty hands. Everything on this list gets to 60mph in under four seconds!

It's quite **quick.**

Pagani Zonda F

Engine: *V12*

Power: *685bhp*

Top speed: *214mph*

0-60mph: *3.5s*

TG power lap: *1 min 18.4s*

Richard loves this deranged machine. Light, nimble and more slippery than a greased torpedo, the F stands for Fangio, the legendary racing driver who helped develop it. If you've never heard of him, just pretend it stands for 'fast'.

Welcome to the **dark side!**

Bugatti Veyron

Engine: *W16 quad turbocharged*

Power: *1001bhp*

Top speed: *253mph*

0-60mph: *2.5s*

TG power lap: *Not tested*

The Veyron is stupendous in every way: check out its price tag! It's faster than an F1 car and puts out enough power to heat Belgium (and with 10 radiators, it probably could). James tested its top speed and made it to 252.9mph.

Ariel Atom

Engine: *4-cylinder supercharged*

Power: *300bhp*

Top speed: *140mph*

0-60mph: *2.9s*

TG power lap: *1 min 19.5s*

Driving **nirvana.**

The hugely enjoyable Atom is built by one of the world's smallest car companies – and from about eight parts. There's an engine, seats, four wheels and not much else. It's ultra-light and so fast, it will reshape your face – because it doesn't even have a windscreen.

Completely mad. **Raw, vicious** unbridled **power.**

Koenigsegg CCX

Engine: *V8, twin supercharged*

Power: *850bhp*

Top speed: *250mph*

0-60mph: *3.2s*

TG power lap: *1 min 17.6s*

It's loud, Swedish and made entirely of unobtainium (OK, carbon fibre). It tried to kill The Stig, but after Koenoegsoenginegger (or however you spell it) tamed it with a spoiler, The Stig and the CCX fell in love. One of the fastest cars ever to go around Top Gear's track.

Lamborghini Murciélago LP640

Engine: *V12*

Power: *640bhp*

Top speed: *211mph*

0-60mph: *3.4s*

TG power lap: *1 min 19.8s*

Sure, its doors open upwards instead of outwards, but by Lamborghini standards, this missile is pretty normal. The name means 'bat' in Spanish, and it does indeed go like a bat... out of hell. But the handling isn't devilish, thanks to 4WD.

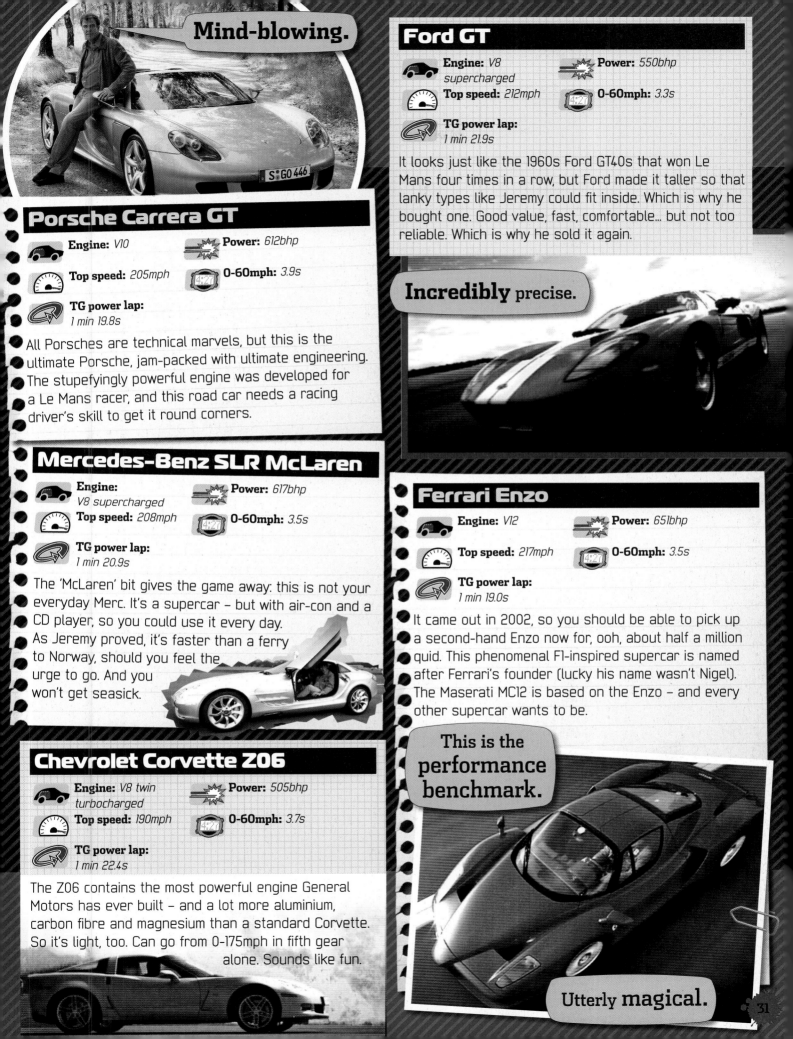

Mind-blowing.

Ford GT

Engine: V8 supercharged
Power: 550bhp
Top speed: 212mph
0-60mph: 3.3s
TG power lap: 1 min 21.9s

It looks just like the 1960s Ford GT40s that won Le Mans four times in a row, but Ford made it taller so that lanky types like Jeremy could fit inside. Which is why he bought one. Good value, fast, comfortable... but not too reliable. Which is why he sold it again.

Porsche Carrera GT

Engine: V10
Power: 612bhp
Top speed: 205mph
0-60mph: 3.9s
TG power lap: 1 min 19.8s

All Porsches are technical marvels, but this is the ultimate Porsche, jam-packed with ultimate engineering. The stupefyingly powerful engine was developed for a Le Mans racer, and this road car needs a racing driver's skill to get it round corners.

Incredibly precise.

Mercedes-Benz SLR McLaren

Engine: V8 supercharged
Power: 617bhp
Top speed: 208mph
0-60mph: 3.5s
TG power lap: 1 min 20.9s

The 'McLaren' bit gives the game away: this is not your everyday Merc. It's a supercar – but with air-con and a CD player, so you could use it every day. As Jeremy proved, it's faster than a ferry to Norway, should you feel the urge to go. And you won't get seasick.

Ferrari Enzo

Engine: V12
Power: 651bhp
Top speed: 217mph
0-60mph: 3.5s
TG power lap: 1 min 19.0s

It came out in 2002, so you should be able to pick up a second-hand Enzo now for, ooh, about half a million quid. This phenomenal F1-inspired supercar is named after Ferrari's founder (lucky his name wasn't Nigel). The Maserati MC12 is based on the Enzo – and every other supercar wants to be.

This is the performance benchmark.

Chevrolet Corvette Z06

Engine: V8 twin turbocharged
Power: 505bhp
Top speed: 190mph
0-60mph: 3.7s
TG power lap: 1 min 22.4s

The Z06 contains the most powerful engine General Motors has ever built – and a lot more aluminium, carbon fibre and magnesium than a standard Corvette. So it's light, too. Can go from 0-175mph in fifth gear alone. Sounds like fun.

Utterly magical.

True or False?

Top Gear helped design the Koenigsegg CCX supercar.	**1**	T F
Jeremy Clarkson is the only Top Gear presenter who doesn't own a Porsche.	**2**	T F
James May has a pet ferret named Fiat.	**3**	T F
Jeremy Clarkson's first job was selling Rupert the Bear toys.	**4**	T F
Jeremy Clarkson was once forced to eat his own hair on Top Gear.	**5**	T F
Richard Hammond once presented the Crufts dog show.	**6**	T F
Richard Hammond hates celery.	**7**	T F
James May, who has a degree in music, wrote the Top Gear theme music.	**8**	T F
You can drive round the Top Gear test track on a video game.	**9**	T F
The Stig once answered a mobile phone.	**10**	T F

Jeremy, James and Richard have each bought a cheap Italian supercar and have to drive it to a nightclub. All of them will break down before the finish, but who gets closest?

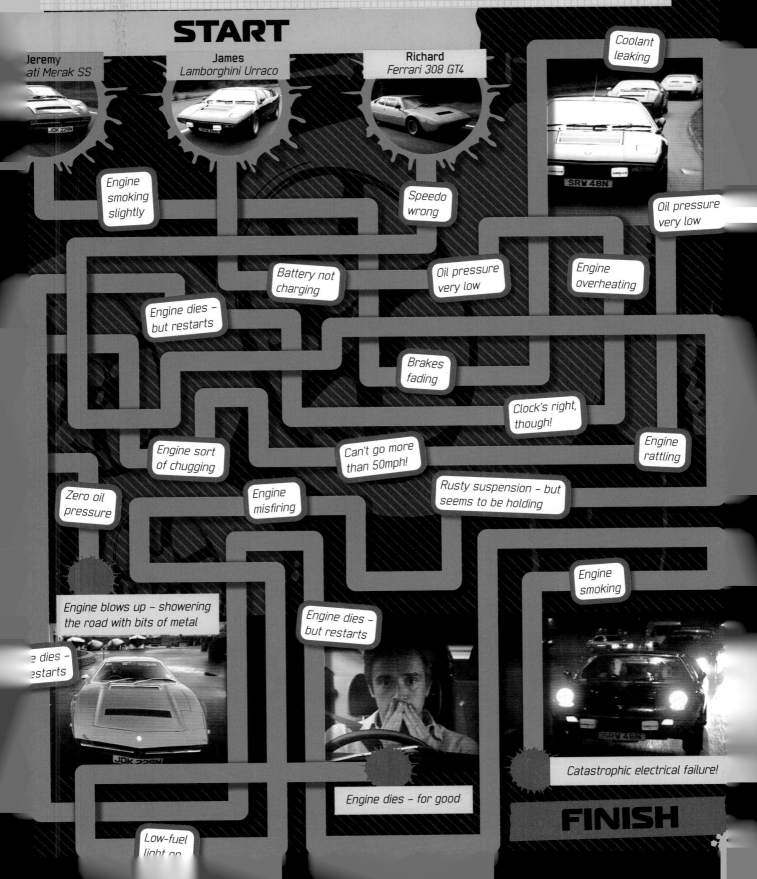

START

Jeremy
ati Merak SS

James
Lamborghini Urraco

Richard
Ferrari 308 GT4

Coolant leaking

Engine smoking slightly

Speedo wrong

Oil pressure very low

Battery not charging

Oil pressure very low

Engine overheating

Engine dies – but restarts

Brakes fading

Clock's right, though!

Engine sort of chugging

Can't go more than 50mph!

Engine rattling

Zero oil pressure

Engine misfiring

Rusty suspension – but seems to be holding

Engine smoking

Engine blows up – showering the road with bits of metal

Engine dies – but restarts

e dies – estarts

Engine dies – for good

Catastrophic electrical failure!

FINISH

Low-fuel light on

Your Fantasy Family Car

There probably isn't a supercar on your driveway. There's probably something really dull with wipe-clean seats and 109 handy storage compartments. Just imagine what you could do to make your family ride a bit cooler – using stuff you've probably already got lying around the house!*

Periscope

Bonnet Scoop

Racing Stripes

Whitewall tyres

Bonnet Scoop
This will make your car look exactly like a drag racer. Simply glue one of the big nozzles from an old vacuum cleaner to the bonnet. Use very strong glue.

Racing Stripes
These are guaranteed to make the car go faster. Simply use any paint that's lying around in the shed. Not brown, though: that colour will make the car slower.

Lower Ride
Lowriders are still pretty cool. Unfortunately they take quite a bit of welding and engineering work, but you can get the same effect just by loading up the car with bricks.

* WARNING: unless you want to get grounded for 20 years, don't actually try any of this nonsense!

Periscope

Owners of 4WDs are always boasting about how they can look out over the traffic from the high-up driving position. Knock together a periscope from a couple of make-up mirrors and get the same effect!

CD of Ferrari Effects

Stick this CD of Ferrari engine noises in the CD player and turn it up loud enough to drown out the feeble real engine noise.

Subwoofers

Simply photocopy a speaker a few times and stick the copies all over the inside of the car to convince the world you've got the world's loudest stereo.

Subwoofer Bricks

3 Spoilers COOL!

Rocket Power

Spoiler

This has to be huge, or no one will take you seriously. Try screwing a small bookshelf to the bootlid: the three-storey spoiler effect is bound to impress.

Rocket Propulsion

Bonfire Night fireworks just won't do the job here, so ask your friendly local rocket scientist to give you something with more oomph. Using lots of very strong tape, stick the rockets to the floor of the boot. Leave the bootlid open, or they won't work very well when you fire them up. Also, be careful not to melt the car behind you.

Big exhaust

Big Exhaust

Embarrassed by the size of your pipe? Just get an old paint can, cut a hole in the bottom and push over the end to get that big-exhaust effect.

Whitewall Tyres

It's about time these came back into fashion. Once you've practised on the racing stripes, painting a white circle should be dead easy.

The Top Gear crew have their own private test track, where they've broken all sorts of cars and caravans and rockets in their attempts to break records.

Fastest caravan

James organises a record attempt on the caravan-towing world land speed record: currently 128.86mph. A Mitsubishi Evo VII is the tow car. But the driver only makes it to 125.2mph before the caravan starts to fall apart. Then the car's engine blows up. James punishes the caravan by dropping it from a big crane.

GOING...

GOING...

GONE!

Fastest star in a reasonably priced car

The Chevrolet Lacetti's name rhymes with 'settee' and it's only slightly faster than one. Still, Top Gear's celebrity guests try to drive a Lacetti round the test track as fast as possible. Topping the leader board is X Factor judge Simon Cowell at 1 min 45.9s.

Fastest rockety thing

It was a big project: to create a reusable space vehicle from a Reliant Robin. It was ambitious, and yes, it did end in a fiery wreck. But it did leave the ground, making it the largest non-commercial rocket launch in European history.

Fastest car on the runway

Top Gear's test facility is based at an airfield, so it has a runway – which is great for testing top speeds. Unless you're in a supercar, because you still run out of road (and nerve) before you reach the limit. So what's the fastest anyone's driven down it? The answer: Jeremy in the Koenigsegg CCX, reaching 193mph.

BRAKE

In here, no-one can hear you scream.

Most rolls

So, this isn't a speed record – or a sandwich-eating record. It was an attempt to beat the record for most complete rolls in a car... with someone inside it. The car was a 1991 Ford Sierra. Sierras were once common on British roads; after this stunt, there's one less of them. Five rolls was the figure to beat; TG's stunt driver managed six!

Fastest car... indoors

To go fast indoors, you need a really, really big building, like the Excel arena in London's Docklands. It's 385m long. A quick car is also useful: how about a 900hp Toyota F1 car? It can do 220mph (outdoors). After a test run in Top Gear's Chevrolet Lacetti (70mph), The Stig climbed into the racing car and gave it the beans. The result: a mere 81mph. Pretty bad, but the floor was too slippery. It's still a world record though!

Panasonic

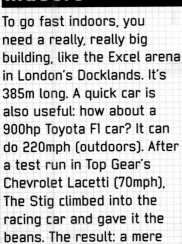

BA-DOOM

Swamps and Highways

The challenge:

Drive across Alabama state lines without being yelled at by the locals. Easy enough? Well, Richard, Jeremy and James have managed to enrage a delightful group of rednecks who have decided to take them on.

Help deliver the lads across the state line in one piece by cutting out a playing piece, grabbing some die and completing this hairy, scary game.

Rough rules:

Watch out for the swamps. Hit one of those suckers and you're back to where it starts. On the other hand, if you land on a square with a highway, follow it to the square on which it ends. The first one to cross the state line is the winner. Yee-haa!

20 19 18

21

22

23 24 25

44 43 42

45

46

47

48 49 50

I'm doing something I **never** thought I'd do – I'm **running**

Thrashed

There's always been a spot of smashing, crashing and thrashing on Top Gear. OK, so some of it may be a bit pointless, but it's fun!

Bullseye

Take two slightly mad presenters and put them in a quarry with six battered bangers. Add a nitrogen powered canon, throw in a caravan for good measure and, ladies and gentlemen, you have all ingredients needed for a game of car darts!

FWAP

That's the **coolest** thing I've ever seen!

Richard the conkerer

Caravan-lovers look away now.

This 'game' was loosely based on the old playground favourite, conkers. Just replace the small nuts with six mobile homes.

Huge cranes hoisted the caravans high above the ground before one was released and allowed to swing down and smash into the other.

Blown away

This is possibly the silliest stunt the Top Gear team ever pulled! The idea was to see how a car would cope with the crosswinds caused by a Virgin 747 jet – an everyday hazard faced by most motorists, of course.

First up was a Ford Mondeo, which was sent hurtling 50 feet backwards by the plane's thrust. It never stood a chance. The blast from the engines sent the car flipping over and over, until it finally came to rest in a mangled heap.

Big engine, lightweight hippy **car. This** should be **fun.**

We're grown **men** playing **conkers** with **caravans.**

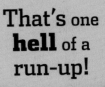

That's one **hell** of a run-up!

Wedding wows...

Another mad Top Gear stunt set about seeing whether a 26ft stretch limo, weighing in at some 3 tonnes, could 'jump' over an outdoor wedding party. Oh, and a few caravans and assorted manky motors.

Well, it did clear the wedding reception, and actually made it over one of the 'sacrificial' caravans too. But then it nosedived and before the bride could say 'I do' was heading for that great scrap yard in the sky.

Frying tonight

The Top Gear team had been on the hunt for the world's worst car. Richard found it in the Nissan Sunny.

He set out to get revenge by placing it directly behind a dragster. A flick of a switch, a whirring of jet engines and a burst of flames, and suddenly the ugly Nissan was history!

Not that Richard took it all out on the Nissan. Oh no, he torched a caravan too, just for good measure!

This **commits** the **worst crime** of all – **blandness.**

RRMMMBLL

RRMMMBLL
RRMMMBLL

FIREFORCE

RRMMMBLL

Mashed Maserati

Now, Jeremy loves Maseratis. In fact he claims he could say Maserati before he could say mummy.

But what he didn't like was a Maserati Biturbo that he bought. He hated it so much that he decided to drop a skip full of rubbish right on top of it!

It got what it deserved because it was an affront to one of the best badges in the businesses.

CRRUMMP

FFOOOM

How much **fun** was that!

41

Some say every Stig has his day. However, nobody, least of all the man in white, expected that day to involve skidding off the Top Gear test track for a high speed tiptoe through the tyre wall. But that's exactly what happened when our tame racing driver got a little too fresh with a visitor from Sweden – the Koenigsegg CCX.

Revisit that special afternoon by completing the word search puzzle below and remember with fondness how, for a few thrilling seconds, the mighty 'White Stig' became 'The White Stig With Brown Streaks'.

```
S E M X N V H Z U N E O G O H T L I S
A O Q M Y T G F N E J N T E Y O H L T
U S A E R R M S E N I I J E L R I T H
C P I Z I I L E C D F K D F A O I T I
R I R W I G D S D P O L C I O L A L F
Y N S C M Q O I G Z E R O A P L E E E
D N X Q E N K N P M T F F T E S D Y Y
G I T O H S I O L L A W E R Y T E A X
D N N O Y K U N D E R S T E E R H I F
T G I O A I P P O W E R F U L S N A T
X G B R M F E H E S L E E W C R L R O
S Y B N E I A L H R E E P C E O M O L
E R B I F N O B R A C T X E O M N C O
G C L I D S R R C R C H T E D V K E T
M L Z L T O P O O A A S A T E E L T A
C N I I B J M F C P R H E R P L M I P
C N T X G X N R S E T L O S G A H T H
G E E P O W A S V G N I H C E E R C S
M W C B O S N O I T C U R T S E D F W
H O W D H I G H N P B L X F E G I S C
```

Tyre wall	Cornering	Screeching	Spinning
Supercharged	Downforce	Handling	Mayhem
Oversteer	Lost It	Carbon Fibre	Accelerate
CCX	Oh No!	Skidding	Crash
Understeer	Powerful	Destruction	Braking

Gotcha!

Start

Eastmere in Norfolk is a purpose-built village, used by the British Army to train soldiers in urban warfare. It's also not a bad place to take potshots at Jeremy in a Mercedes SLK 55 AMG. While James and Richard volunteered, it was decided to leave it to the Irish Guards to do the firing.

Jeremy did quite well, being caught in the crosshairs only 13 times. Now it's your turn to try your luck. See if you can get through the village without ending up as Swiss cheese.

Finish

Top 10 Grown-up Cars

You know how it is. You really want a supercar, but you also need something big and comfy with four doors, so you can run Granny and Grandpa down to the bingo. Really fast.

BMW M5

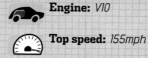

Engine: V10 **Power:** 500bhp
Top speed: 155mph **0-60mph:** 4.7s

The 7-Series BMW is plusher and almost any other car is less ugly, but if you want a four-door Beemer, Five is the magic number: 5.0 litres, 500bhp and 500mph (well, nearly).

Audi A8

Engine: V8 diesel **Power:** 322bhp
Top speed: 155mph **0-60mph:** 5.9s

Low-key luxury for people who don't want to be labelled Merc or BMW owners. The diesel version's almost as fast as the W12 but loads cheaper. (Yes, we like the diesel!)

Jaguar XJR

Engine: V8 **Power:** 400bhp
Top speed: 155mph **0-60mph:** 5s

Yes, we know you'd rather have the XK, but you can get an XJR for less money and it's faster. The body's all aluminium, so it won't rust if you leave it out in the rain. That's handy.

Bentley Continental Flying Spur

Engine: W12 **Power:** 552bhp
Top speed: 195mph **0-60mph:** 4.9s

All right, it looks a bit odd and stretched. But it's a Bentley. And it's pretty expensive. And it's a Bentley. And that stonking engine is the one we told you not to put in your Audi A8. And it's a Bentley.

Maserati Quattroporte GT

Engine: V8 **Power:** 400bhp
Top speed: 167mph **0-60mph:** 5.6s

Quattroporte just means 'four doors', but it sounds so much better in Italian, eh? So does the exhaust note. A beautiful car, and rarer than the German executive saloons.

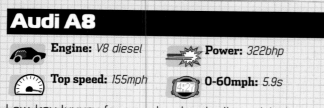

Rolls-Royce Phantom

Engine: V12 **Power:** 453bhp

Top speed: 149mph **0-60mph:** 5.7s

Its styling might have been inspired by a brick, but somehow it works. Huge, luxurious and mind-bogglingly expensive, this is the car for those who think a Mercedes S-Class is a bit cheap and nasty.

Mercedes-Benz S500

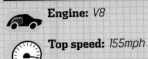

Engine: V8 **Power:** 388bhp

Top speed: 155mph **0-60mph:** 5.6s

You want gadgets you never knew existed? Then buy an S-Class. The S65 AMG version has over 600bhp but it's limited to the same top speed.

Porsche Cayenne

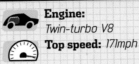

Engine: Twin-turbo V8 **Power:** 493bhp

Top speed: 171mph **0-60mph:** 5.1s

Porsche purists burst into tears when a Cayenne passes them in the street. A Porsche SUV? The horror! OK, you wouldn't go racing in it, but it's still Porsche-quick and luxurious enough.

Range Rover Vogue SE

Engine: V8 diesel **Power:** 268bhp

Top speed: 124mph **0-60mph:** 9.2s

You want a luxury car. You want it at the top of that mountain there. The original and best posh 4WD is the car for you. Buy the diesel model, so the fuel costs don't make your eyes water... so much.

Vauxhall VXR8

Engine: V8 **Power:** 411bhp

Top speed: 195mph **0-60mph:** 4.9s

It's not the most luxurious car here, but it's half the price of anything else. This Australian-built monster is the joker in this pack – especially if your idea of a joke is going round every corner sideways.

That's Not Gone Well

You know how when we do these **big** things, they usually end in a **massive** disaster...?

The Top Gear crew plan some great stunts and challenges. Only sometimes, they don't plan them quite well enough.

Cars as boats

The challenge was to make an amphibious vehicle. Jeremy fastened an outboard motor to a Toyota pick-up, Richard turned a VW camper van into a canal boat, while James stuck a mast on an old Triumph Herald. Sadly, the Damper Van sank and the Toybota capsized. But the Herald made it.

Cars as boats II

They failed to learn their lesson, and tried again – this time across the English Channel. Damper Van II sank again, so did the Herald, but Jeremy's Nissank – a Nissan with an outboard this time – actually made the crossing.

GLUG GLUG GLUG GLUG GLUG GLUG

Caravan holiday

When the Top Gear boys – all caravan haters – went on a mini-break to Dorset, we feared for the caravan's life. James crashed it into a bollard, then Jeremy accidentally burnt it to the ground while trying to cook chips.

Space shuttle

James and Richard tried launching a Reliant Robin into space. Unfortunately, the Reliant proved just as rubbish in flight as it is on the road. Instead of gliding back to earth for re-use, it crashed in a fireball.

BA-DOOM

Limousines

Our three heroes had to build their own stretch limos, then deliver three music stars to the BRIT Awards in London. James got lost, Richard's throttle got stuck and Jeremy's car was too long to go round corners – but then it snapped in half, solving that problem.

Convertible people carrier

James, Richard and Jeremy used their engineering and sewing skills to create a soft-topped Renault Espace. It just about survived rigorous testing until they tried driving it through a brand new £1 million automatic car wash, which caught fire.

Just run!

47

The Super Quiz
– it's stupidly hard

Right, so you think you know about Top Gear? Reckon you've got a good grasp of cars and an encyclopaedic knowledge of every episode we've ever filmed?

Well try this lot for size. We'll give you two points for a right answer and laugh at you every time you get one wrong.

And then at the end we'll tell you how rubbish you really are.

Enjoy!

1 You've seen the Stig hammer round it on countless occasions, but what's the name of the second from last corner on the Top Gear test track?

A. Gambon   **B.** Bacharach   **C.** Chicago

2 Now Jezza loves his supercars but can you remember which one he compared to a prawn and avocado sandwich?

A. Bugatti Veyron

B. Ford GT

C. Mercedes McLaren SLR

3 Britain has Racing Green, while Italy favours red for its racing cars. But which colour did the Germans pick?

A. Pink   **B.** Yellow   **C.** Silver

4 What edible delight played a key role in the race between Jeremy, in a Bugatti Veyron, and Richard and James, in their little plane?

A. a trifle   **B.** a truffle   **C.** a triffid

5 Which car was struck by lightning with Richard still inside it?

A. Mini Cooper   **B.** Ford Escort   **C.** VW Golf

6 Costing just under £900,000, which car did the Top Gear team vote as the 'maddest car in the world'?

A. Rinspeed Splash

B. Ariel Atom

C. Noble M12 GTO

7 How many times did Steve the Stuntman roll his Ford Sierra in order to make it into the Guinness Book of Records?

A. Two   **B.** Four   **C.** Six

8 Who had 'Country and Western is rubbish' daubed across their car during the US special?

A. James   **B.** Jeremy   **C.** Richard

9 Richard broke all the rules when he gave his Opel Kadett a name during the trek across Botswana. Can you remember what he called it?

A. Stanley   **B.** Oliver   **C.** Harold

10 Which car was considered so cool that instead of a place on the Cool Wall (R.I.P.) it was actually given it's own little fridge?

A. Aston Martin DBS   **B.** Ferrari Enzo

C. Porsche Carrera GT

11 In which country is the Milau super bridge, the scene of some gratuitous boy racing when the team crossed it in three supercars?

A. Ireland   **B.** France   **C.** Italy

12 What's different about Stig's American cousin?

A. He wears pink   **B.** He's got a big belly
C. He is actually a she

13 To the nearest fiver, how much does a Eurofighter Typhoon cost?

A. £12 million   **B.** £65 million   **C.** £1 billion

14 Ferrari love the Enzo, but who or what did they name it after?

A. The company's founder
B. The company's cat
C. The company's bank manager

15 As well as pride and a bit of skill, the threat of a lift home in what car kept the trio going in their race across Botswana?

A. Fiat Panda   **B.** VW Beetle   **C.** Austin Allegro

16 Which presenter only got the job because of his lustrous hair?

A. James   **B.** The Stig   **C.** Jeremy

17 Driving the Lacetti, who is the fastest female Star in a Reasonably Priced Car?

A. Dame Helen Mirren   **B.** Jennifer Saunders
C. Billie Piper

18 What award did the Kia Cerato win in 2006?

A. Caravan Club Towing Car of the Year
B. Sony Best Sounding Horn of the Decade
C. The Wipe-eze Fastest Windscreen Wipers of the Century

19 OK, so you all know a Reliant Robin has got three wheels, but can you spot the other hub cap-challenged 'marque' out of these three?

A. Heinkel   **B.** Fokker   **C.** Messerschmitt

20 As a punishment for moonlighting as a presenter on daytime TV, Richard was sent out to drive which bright pink car?

A. Nissan Micra   **B.** Suzuki Liana   **C.** Triumph Herald

TURN TO PAGE 92 FOR THE ANSWERS

37+ points
You're a Ferrari

You're either so clever that you should be presenting Top Gear or a sneaky cheat. We think you cheated, so you're disqualified.

31–36 points
You're a Porsche

A good attempt. Methodical, measured but lacking that bit of passion, that touch of flair to get you to the top. Keep trying.

21–30 points
You're a Ford Escort

You're dull but reliable. You do just enough to scrape by but you really need to aim higher. And lose those furry dice.

11–20 points
You're a Lada

After they made you, they threw away the mould. Let's face it, guess work got you through.

0–10 points
You're a caravan

You're so bad you haven't even got an engine. Hang your head in shame.

Indes-truck-tible!

How to ALMOST destroy a Hilux in 8 simple steps.

Subject: Toyota Hilux pick-up truck

Age: 13 years

Cost: About £1,000

Miles: 190,000

Condition: Shabby. Indications of dirt, rust and dents in most areas of the car suggest the Hilux spent most of its life off the road.

Conclusion: Life's been hard for the Hilux. And it's only going to get harder...

Step 1:

The Great Bristol Stair Test

Obviously fooled by its rustic appearance, Jeremy decided that running the Hilux down several flights of cold, hard, stone steps in Bristol would pose a challenge for the veteran pick-up. Aside from giving the vehicle's suspension a bit of a tickle, the only real damage was to Jeremy's spine. You're just hurting yourself, Clarkson...

Step 2:

Hilux vs Tree

... and now you're hurting our green friends. Disappointed by the lack of harm being done to the Hilux through the scraping, nudging, bashing and general hitting of assorted inanimate objects, Jeremy decided to run the car, at considerable speed, into a tree.

Once again, the Hilux, despite some superficial damage, shrugged off the encounter. The tree on the other hand (a delightful 30-year-old horse chestnut just minding its own business), was left with a sizeable dent that was later blamed on local vandals. Jeremy and the Hilux, oblivious to the injustice, continued on their merry way...

Step 3:

Where not to park a Hilux

That would be on the boat ramp at the Severn Estuary just before high tide – the second biggest tide in the world.

Battered by waves and eventually drowned in corrosive salt water, the Hilux resisted a rescue attempt by local divers, eventually reappearing five hours later when the monster tide receded. Jeremy, convinced that this was the end of the Hilux, gave it a final pat and trudged off to the pub; only to be stopped by the sound of the engine ticking over and roaring (with a few wet splutters) back to life. Witnesses at the scene claim Jeremy shed tears of joy. He swears it was just a bit of sea spray.

E473 CJN

Step 4, 5 & 6:

Hilux vs Top Gear production office vs caravan vs wrecking ball

All presumably solid, hurty-type objects; all utterly useless against the bafflingly tough Hilux.

Top Gear production office: the Hilux performed like a knife through butter. Hilux: 1, Office: nil.

Caravan: The team continued its campaign of abuse against the popular recreational vehicle, (dropping one from a great height onto the Hilux) knowing full well the effect this would have, i.e. none at all.

Wrecking ball: has since retired in shame.

Step 7:

If at first you don't succeed...

... set fire to it and go home. That's just plain mean.

Step 8:

But wait, there's more!

Enter James May. Calculating and cold-blooded, James surmised that, logically, since all ground level attempts at destroying the Hilux had failed, a vertical approach was bound to succeed.

So James set it on the roof of a tower block in East London and then had the building spectacularly demolished.

As smoke and debris filled the air, spectators eagerly awaited the outcome. Would the Hilux be buried under thousands of pounds of public housing? Crumpled and crushed beyond all recognition?
Never again to enjoy the feel of bitumen beneath its unroadworthy tyres?

On the 7th of December, 2003, the Toyota Hilux, having been rammed, rattled, drowned, smashed, bashed, torched and, finally, demolished, was driven into the Top Gear studios to a hero's welcome. Today it sits proudly on a plinth, as both a tribute to the mighty pick-up and a memorial to all those that have suffered at the hands of berks with nothing better to do than victimise honest, hard-working vehicles. And chestnut trees.

They **look** as if they've **nicked** something!

Cars vs

James is racing his Peugeot 207 against some blokes in silly trousers who can leap across buildings, fences, benches – in fact anything that gets in their way! Trace the lines below and find out which one DOESN'T lead to the finish.

START

FINISH

Blokes

Two years after taking on the runny-jumpy guys, James went to Budapest to challenge two scallywags on BMX bikes to a race – this time in a new Fiat 500. Can you put these nine pictures in the right order?

This stunt was done by a **professional stunt team** who trained for **100 years**. Do **not** even **think** about trying this at home!

Fox vs Aygo Footy

Wouldn't football be even cooler with cars tearing up the pitch? Top Gear certainly thought so and decided to host its very own small-car soccer match with Toyota Aygos against Volkswagen Foxes!

> My **one** worry is that after seeing this, people aren't going to be **bothered** about watching the **real** World Cup!

Brazil

Foxes

Czech Republic

Aygoes

With seconds to go till kick-off, James and Richard square up to each other. Both are number one for their teams and both badly want to win this. May is with the Aygos which are made in the Czech Republic. Hammond's playing on the Fox team, whose cars are built in Brazil. If real footy's anything to go by, you might think the Foxes have already got it in the bag!

James wins the toss, and decides to let the Foxes kick off. The Brazilian skill is immediately obvious, with some neat swerves giving them possession of the ball early on.

May makes a cheeky interception and is heading for the undefended Fox goal. But the Brazilians are bigger and tackle hard!

SCREEEEECH!

> Oh, you **fouled!**

Soon, the Aygos' ability shines through and they begin to dominate the game. A cool header from Aygo 2 sets things up nicely for Aygo 4 which drives the ball into the net.

James can't help annoying Richard, who's less than pleased to be lagging behind so early on in the match.

Richard reminds his team they have good qualities, but speed off the line isn't one of them! It's a weakness that the Aygos take full advantage of, though. Aygo 2 nips in to gain possession and passes to Aygo 4 which whips round and plants it straight into the goal. It's 2-nil to the Agyos and disaster for the Foxes!

1-0

Ya-haaaaa!

That, mate, was a **magnificent,** choreographed goal...

Yes, yes, yes, yes, yes...!

Beep! Beep! Beep!

2-0

KRUMP!

Desperate to make a comeback, the Brazilians will stop at nothing to gain control of the ball. Tempers fray as the cars smash into each other like dodgems. The drivers seem to have forgotten though that they haven't got big, rubber bumpers to stop them getting bashed in!

The Foxes fumble with the ball near the Agyos' goal, and pray for just one goal before half-time. Too late! The horn sounds and Richard looks like he's going to cry.

55

Before the second half kicks off, both teams check out how many dents, cracks and scratches they've suffered. If these were real footy players, not cars, they'd all have had broken legs by now and been carried off on stretchers!

Half time

It's the second half, and boy, the Foxes certainly have a mountain to climb.

S)CREEEECH!

S)CREEEECH!

The Aygos' are on the ball again, but it rolls over James' roof and a cunning Fox gets in there. The Brazilians keep it up, dribbling past the Agyos' defence, which is all over the place!

Fox 2 brushes off the Aygos' with a scorching run, and plants it in the back of the net! It's now 2-1 to the Czechs, but at least Richard's got something to smile about at last!

GOAAAAAAAL!

2-1

2-2

There's no stopping them now. The Foxes are getting into their stride and quickly bag the equaliser making it 2-all. Richard's so happy, his head's about to explode!

Then, following an Aygo foul, the Foxes are given a free kick. The ball ricochets off an Aygo roof and straight into the net. Textbook goal! It's 3-2 to Brazil.

Free kick!

3-2

KRUMP!

OOF!

KRUMP!

With full time approaching fast, the game really hots up. A fight breaks out leaving May's car seriously injured, but it carries on like a true pro. Other Aygos' take a pounding too, but they're not beaten yet...

With just minutes to go; the Aygos bag another goal, making it 3-all!

The crowd's going mad, (well, the Top Gear camera crew are, anyway). There's just seconds left and the only way the Foxes can get the better of the agile Aygos is to smash them out of the way!

3-3

Oh **yes!**

It's Richard versus Aygo 4 down the wing. He loses the ball, but number 6 comes out of nowhere to ram it home. The horn goes for full time and Richard's done it! They were well down in the first half, but the Foxes beat the Aygos 4-3!

3-4

Full time!

How to Spot a Car

Expert!

Do you know someone who you reckon is a bit of a geek when it comes to cars? If you can answer yes to these six questions, then chances are, he is!

01 Is he always coming out with big words and long-winded explanations that he knows full well are going to confuse you?

It measures the wheel **horsepower**, and then, by letting it run down, it **converts** the mechanical **drag** into the extra **horsepower** in the **flywheel.**

Er... good!

02 Does he get annoyed with people who don't know as much about cars as he does?

Eh? No, it's **not** a kit car. It's a Lamborghini. You **philistine!**

03 Does he think he can tell if someone's car is rubbish just by looking at it?

I **know** about **old cars**, as you know, and I **can look** at this with my **trained** eye, and can **tell you** immediately that it's a **pup!**

05 Does he draw really rubbish car diagrams he thinks are great, even when nobody else does?

This is my **detailed** engineering drawing of what I think we can do. **This bit** at the back is on **a frame,** and then **in the middle,** I'm proposing this removable **hoop!**

06 Does he like to tell you stories about all his car heroes that might actually be interesting if they didn't last half an hour?

Hmm...

There's this **racing driver** here called **Woolf Barnato.** Someone **challenged** him to get **from Cannes to England** in the time it took the **Blue Train** to get from **Cannes to Calais**...

By the way, we think we just might have a car nerd on Top Gear – any idea who it might be?

May's Maze

How hard can it be?

J ames May is famous for having a terrible sense of direction. What's more, he's driving an old car with a steering problem and he can't turn left. Ever. Can you guide him through this maze? If you take the shortest route, the letters you'll pass will spell a phrase.

Remember, no left turns!

D S N Q T

H E R   E

V U W

L   G   I   D

L   Y   M   A

E   U

A   X   N

W   I   O

T T C O   S   E

T   F   D   G   FINISH

L N   C

K   I   START

Spot the Stig

The Stig. He's 100% quick. Some say he does actually speak but his words are twice the speed of sound so come out too fast to hear. And when he's behind the wheel, he's impossible to catch – even on film. Can you match the blurred images below with the car that The Stig is driving?

A

B

1

2

C

D

3

E

4

F

RX53 KHP

6

5

SURVIVAL TIPS

Faced with an extreme situation, you can't always rely on airbags and anti-lock brakes to save your skin. Here are some Top Gear top tips for surviving...

01. Drowning

Just driven into a swimming pool? It's easily done. Jeremy survived the experience, Richard almost didn't. Generally, try to get out of the car ASAP, or you'll have to wait till it hits the bottom and has finished filling with water. Which takes patience and big lungs.

02. Rioting

So you find yourself in a country where society is breaking down, or at Hamleys on sale day. What you need is a Talon riot control vehicle. It's armour-plated, electrified and has a grenade launcher... and most importantly, an inside loo.

03. Africa

Loads of sand here, so drive something lightweight, such as a VW Beetle or a 1963 Opel Kadett. Loads of fierce animals, too, such as lions, snakes and, um, honey badgers, so under no circumstances throw away your car doors to save weight – unless you're Jeremy and James.

1 Just get **out** as **fast** as you can.

2

3 Why don't **all** cars have **no doors?** When I **come** to **power,** I'm going to make it a **rule,** cos this is just **better.**

04. Lightning

There are dark clouds overhead, the sound of the thunder. More ominous yet, the weather forecast is 'fine and sunny'. Yep, you're about to be struck by lightning. Don't worry, Richard got hit by 800,000 volts in a car and survived. Just keep your hands away from any exposed metal.

05. High altitude

Jeremy proved that all you need for mountaineering is a can of fizzy drink, a can of soup, some diesel (to start a fire to heat up the soup) and a Land Rover Discovery. Using this combination, he scaled Cnoc an Fhreiceadain in Scotland – a mountain as hard to pronounce as it is to climb.

4 KRAK! KRAK! KRAK!

06. Haunting

Richard and James survived a night in Screaming Woods in Pluckley, 'the most haunted village in England' sleeping in a Smart ForFour. The ghosts kept away – maybe they didn't like the look of the car.

07. Warfare

Jeremy tried escaping a tank in a Range Rover Sport, and failed. He tried avoiding snipers in a Mercedes SLK and a Porsche Boxster, and failed. But he was more successful in avoiding an Apache helicopter gunship in a Lotus Exige. So get one of those.

6

7

Wumpa WUMPA WUMPA WUMPA WUMPA

for those who missed the massive spikey flashy thing telling you about the stunts last time...

Stunts are done by **a professional stunt team** who trained for **100 years. Do not** even think about trying them at **home!**

8

9

ROVER

H566

10

It's **unkillable.**

08. The North Pole

Your fingers can freeze off. The fuel in your car can freeze. Your car can fall through thin ice. Worse still, a polar bear might eat you while you're having a poo. Take a very well prepared 4WD, an Arctic survival course and a big gun, just in case.

09. Espionage

Top Gear proved you can build a James Bond car on a tight budget – £300, to be precise. You'll need some coloured balls (to scatter over the road and confound pursuers), a tea tray (ideally bulletproof), paintball guns, drainpipes (as rocket launchers) and an engineer (to get the tricky ejector seat working).

10. Anything

If you need a vehicle that can survive being washed out to sea, incinerated, crushed by a caravan, crashed into a tree, hit by a wrecking ball or dropped 240 feet on the roof of a building under demolition, you'll need a Toyota Hilux. Just don't be in it.

Small, but Perfectly Formed

Who'd have ever thought Jeremy could get so excited about a small car? The Peel P50 had him literally beside himself with excitement as he whizzed around London with his knees keeping his ears company.

The first challenge was to squeeze his huge 6ft 5 body into a car that's not much bigger than a fridge freezer. In fact, this mini-classic is now listed in the Guinness Book of Records as the smallest production car ever made.

> Leg first and **yes!**

> **Top speed** really depends on how **big** you are and **how** much you had for **breakfast!**

> I can't imagine it's **terribly safe**, especially when your **knees** are the **crumple zones!**

NNNNNNEEEEEEEE EEEEEE EEEEEEEEEEEEEEE

EME 583B

Built on the Isle of Man in 1963 (which makes it six years older than Richard Hammond!) the P50 cost £199 – quite a hefty sum then – but it did do a phenomenal 100 miles to the gallon!

If there was a bonnet, which there isn't, it would hide a 'massive' 4.5 hp engine. Actually the engine is more of a battery nicked from an old moped and it's nestled down by the foot pedals.

Jeremy decides to find out just how good the Peel is as a modern-day city run around, and drives the car to work.

> I have **never** seen the Top Gear team **so enthusiastic** about any car.

> When you **get to work** you just **pick** it up and **carry** it inside!

TOP GEAR
Road Signs
(Because the normal ones don't seem quite up to the job sometimes)

NEVER GIVE WAY

End of Jeremy's drive approaching

Top Gear-approved caravan park

Jeremy Clarkson attempting a fast lap on ice

Maybe you saw The Stig, maybe you didn't

Limousine turning area

Stunt-driving nun ahead

Beware: amphibious cars

Sorry for any delay

20 ZONE

James May navigating in this area

Tall man ahead, wrong side of 40

Escape the City

Jeremy can't wait to test his new supercar, but first he has to escape the city with all its traffic lights and road signs. Can you steer him through this maze? You can only move along roads in the strict sequence green-yellow-red repeatedly.

START

FINISH

DIY Car Darts

What do you mean, you don't have six old bangers, a gas-powered ramjet and a quarry to play in? That's no reason not to play the fine and noble game of car darts.

You will need:

- A friend to play with
- Three toy cars each
- A ruler
- A table
- Er, that's all

How to play:

01 Place this annual on the floor, about 70cm away from a table.

02 Take it in turns to 'drive' a car off the edge of the table, aiming to hit the target.

03 Score points depending on where you land. Hitting the caravan in the centre scores 50 points – high-five your opponent.

04 In case of a draw, measure who got one car nearest the centre. Or play again. And again...

5　10

KKRNTCH

10 WORST CARS

Only One Owner*

Welcome to Top Gear Used Auto Mart, where you'll find a wide selection of (ahem) second-hand motor vehicles. All vehicles come with a money-back guarantee. (We guarantee that once you've bought one of our cars, you'll wish you had your money back.) Feel free to take a look around...

PRE-LOVED

Ford Mondeo
A true single owner vehicle (and he only used it to drive to the airport), this modern, streamlined and aerodynamic Mondeo is noted for its performance in strong wind. Some external damage. Slightly worn Citroen 2CV also available.

Porsche Cayenne Turbo S
Driven mainly on weekends in the relaxing Cypriot countryside, this perfect family vehicle has minor scratching to the front panels which can be easily buffed out. The deployed airbags are due to a minor technical malfunction, and have nothing to do with a man rumoured to be dressed as a flying squirrel who may or may not have jumped out of an airplane in a race against the Porsche. And even if you could prove it, who's going to believe you?

1981 Lancia Beta Coupe
Fantastic city car with proven off-road abilities, the Lancia has modified electrics, variable air-con settings and innovative stylings unique to this particular model. Contact our Botswana showroom for more details.

70

SOME WEAR AND TEAR

Ford Orion
Back of car raised by previous owner and with fuel supply converted to gas, this sporty number really flies. Will throw in a caravan for free.

G-Wiz
Like the Ford Orion, this G-Wiz has also been raised and modified and now boasts fat tyres and 10 times more battery power. All in all an attractive and powerful example of this environmentally-friendly, emission-free car. Note: emission in photo not the fault of manufacturer.

Appliance car
More than adequately holds its own against Korean and Malaysian models in the same class. Plus it'll do a full load of washing and reheat last night's dinner while you drive.

Nissan Sunny
A no-nonsense, no-feature car, this Nissan Sunny is available in a range of colours, including red, burnt sienna and charcoal grey.

WRECKING ONLY

CityRover
Fully functional, roadworthy and ready to drive. This CityRover, however, is too slow even for a man known internationally as Captain Slow. No reasonable offer refused (or unreasonable offers for that matter).

Volkswagen Sharan MPV
Absolutely nothing wrong with this vehicle whatsoever. It is, however, called Sharan.

Caterham Seven Kit Car
These people built it. What do you reckon?

*We guarantee that this small print may be difficult to read.

Africa Challenge

Having proved they could conquer the North Pole, survive the USA and play at Winter Olympics in Lillehammer, Jeremy, James and Richard were challenged to drive 1,000 miles across Botswana.

And the point? To disprove the theory held by people living in Surrey that you need a 4WD because you live up a lane which sometimes has leaves on it. Good luck lads!
(No, really. Good luck...)

It's the **only** Lancia of any sort in the **whole** of Botswana.

You've done well. So **now what?** Do you want a **lift?**

Challenge No.1:

Buy a car for no more than £1,500

So far, so what? The lads had purchased plenty of cheap and reliable cars that could handle difficult, off-road driving conditions. Actually, come to think of it, did we mention the cars can't be 4WDs or be built to go off-road? Oh dear...

Jeremy:
The 1981 Lancia Beta Coupe with bonus cardboard (resting on top of the battery to stop it shorting on the bonnet and starting a fire) at no extra cost!

James:
1985 Mercedes Benz 230E

A car that Africa absolutely **adores** because it's rugged, dependable and **comfortable.**

The Journey

Country: Botswana (which is African for 'appalling driving conditions')

Population: Just over 1.6 million

Living mostly in: Gaborone (the capital) and Francistown

And largely avoiding: The Makgadikgadi Salt Pan, Kalahari Desert and Okavango Delta.

The team's journey: Across the Makgadikgadi Salt Pan, Kalahari Desert and Okavango Delta.

Little-known fact: The Botswana coat of arms features three cog wheels. A celebration of motorization? Since the coat of arms is being held upright by two zebras, we think not. When it comes to driving across 'the spine of Africa', the accepted wisdom is... don't.

> How much more **simple** can you get? It's got **two** moving parts!

Richard:
1963 Opel Kadett

> Where's the **engine?**

They're off!

The three set off and immediately hit their accelerators to give the cars a proper workout. It was at this point the first major disaster of the trip occurred...

... Richard gave his car a name.

The lads were starting to have fun. Richard was enjoying getting acquainted with Oliver. And James and Jeremy were enjoying laughing at him. But the laughter soon stopped, when the tarmac did.

This is just the happiest car in the world. I shall call it 'Oliver'.

He's given it a name!

What is that?

It is collectively our least favourite car in the world. It is the punishment.

Challenge No.2:

The Makgadikadi Salt Pan

As wide as Portugal, almost completely lifeless and untouched by the wheels of any vehicle, let alone cars as rubbish as these, the Makgadikadi was a frightening proposition. But it wasn't the prospect of certain death from lack of food and water that scared Jeremy, James and Richard, it was the possibility that, whosever car broke down, the driver would be faced with completing the journey in... a **Volkswagen Beetle!**

The surface of the Makgadikadi is a wafer-thin salty crust, covering thick, boggy sludge. The lads realised they needed to remove as much weight as possible from their cars before crossing. James and Jeremy took to the task with vigour.

The Weight Shedding Begins...

Richard on the other hand, having formed an emotional attachment to Oliver (let's face it, he was in love), couldn't bring himself to hurt the little car. Though Jeremy offered to help remove Oliver's windows, Richard was certain the car was light enough to make the crossing.

Thanks awfully.

KSSsH!

Oliver is just skipping.

It's very thin glass. Very thin.

Why don't all cars have no doors?

The next day:

Annoyingly, Richard was right. Whatever 'skipping' was, Jeremy and James' cars weren't doing it. More like 'ploughing'... resulting in more weight shedding. And the result of this crash (and smash) diet? Even with the Merc and Lancia looking increasingly like motorcycles, James and Jeremy struggled to stay out of the slime.

While the Beetle waited patiently for its first victim...

RRRRRRR

But the Beetle would have to wait. For the lads survived the 'muck of the Makgadikadi', only to plunge headlong into the 'dust of the... desert'.

And now it's time to play 'Where's Jeremy?'
Can you find Clarkson in the second pic?

Pre-dust

Dust

James wasn't having it any easier. Richard and Oliver, meanwhile, continued on their merry way, dust-free.

Cough! Hack! Splutter!

Finally, the dust ended. To be replaced by dust with rocks. It was at this point that the Lancia decided to take an extended break.

Concerned with the welfare of their friend and fellow traveller, the others left Jeremy to fend for himself.

When Richard and James eventually saw a car approaching in their mirrors, they were sure it would be the Beetle. But somehow, the Lancia, as had all the cars, survived the Makgadikadi, to drive another day...

I'm baaaaaack!

VRROOOMM

That day soon dawned and the three entered the next phase in their African adventure... and with the new day came a new challenge.

The **Kalahari!**

Challenge 3:

Power Laps — Kalahari Style

To see how much power the cars had lost in the Makgadikadi, they were to be tested on a specially constructed Kalahari race track. But it wouldn't be Jeremy, James or Richard driving them. Someone else would be putting the cars (or what was left of them) through their paces. But who?

The Stig's African cousin!

Even without testing them on the Kalahari track, it was plain to see all three cars had lost considerable power. Sadly, the Lancia seemed to have lost not only power, but the will to live. So, the results were not really surprising.

Opel 'Oliver' Kadett: 1 min 12s
Mercedes Benz 230E: 1 min 6s
Lancia Beta Coupe: DNS

Stig's African cousin, not used to sitting still in a stationary car for so long, decided to walk home.

Miraculously though, the Lancia coughed back to life and made it safely to the town of Maun, where the next day, the lads received yet another challenge...

Some say he's seen The Lion King 1,780 times, and that his second best friend is a **cape buffalo.**

I think he was in a **hurry** so he decided **not** to take your car.

77

Challenge 4:

Puny humans vs ferocious animals

James informed the others that they all would be required to drive through the Okavango Delta, home to lions, leopards, cheetahs, hyenas, wild dogs, hippos, black rhinos, crocodiles, bird snakes, shield-nose snakes, puff adders, boomslang, ape cobras, bandit cobras, black mambas, black widows and thick-tailed scorpions – to name just a few.

Given the skeletal conditions of the Lancia and the Merc, James and Jeremy needed to make their cars a little harder to access for the ravenous beasts that awaited them.

For Jeremy, this meant crafting one door from wood, and another from leftover drink cans. Brilliant! Soft aluminium against razor sharp fangs? Shouldn't be an issue.

Comb-over Watch

Deep into the Okavango, the team decided to stop and look at some of the wildlife on show. It provided them with a chance to observe the fascinating 'Americanus Comboverus': A rare species completely oblivious to conventions of good hair styling.

Love your thinking.

Oh man, get it **out!**

That evening, Richard hatched a cunning plan – leave a cow's head in James' tent!

Until Richard discovered that it was in fact his own tent. This not-so-cunning realisation appealed to Jeremy's evil sense of humour.

I do a **fair bit** of offroading... and that's **not** the place to go across.

I've got a **wet bottom!** We're through!

CRASH

Oliveeerrrrr!

Challenge 5:

Cars vs river

Given that they were barely roadworthy, putting the cars through a seaworthiness test, was really pushing the friendship. Nevertheless, James and Jeremy managed to find what they considered a shallow point in the river and prepared to make the crossing. Richard decided to find his own way.

With a little bit of physical encouragement, James and Jeremy made it to the other side.

James and Jeremy were then taught an old Botswanian method for draining water from vehicles. Shoot them.

BLAM BLAM BLAM

You're going to try and **mend** this?

I may need the rifle.

Richard, meanwhile, had found his crossing point. Unfortunately, he forgot to tell Oliver, who decided swimming was a better idea.

Pulled out of the river by a passing tourist bus, the lads inspected the damage to Oliver. Unwilling to accept that Oliver was dead, Richard declared that he could rebuild Oliver.

Richard to the Rescue

Richard knew that if he failed to fix Oliver, he'd have to leave him behind. And that meant completing the rest of the trip in another small German car. And there was no way he was going to let that happen.

The morning brought another hot day but no sign of Richard. Jeremy and James expected the worst. And then the truly miraculous happened...

Oh yeah!

In 47 years I've **never** been speechless.

No **way!**

C'mon! 10 miles!

On the road again

Back on the road, the lads started to taste the hope. And Jeremy and Richard, having exhausted all of their mechanical skills, resorted to an alternative method to keep their cars going. Begging.

And then, something *really* surprising happened.

Oh **no**, not now!

We've done it.

The End!

Meanwhile, James and Richard were celebrating. But they would have to wait to see if Jeremy would be joining them... and in what.

At long last they heard the unmistakable clatter of an air-cooled engine.

WELCOME TO THE
REPUBLIC OF NAMIBIA
60

It's gonna be the Beetle.

And it was...

Yeeaaaaahhhh!!!

...but Jeremy wasn't driving it.

That's astonishing.

Incredibly, all three cars had made it. And so, all that was left to do was to argue about whose car would be awarded overall winner. Despite some rather passionate claims to the title, Jeremy concluded that there could really be only one winner: the **Beetle.**

What?

Top 10 Off-roaders

The boys have, on occasion, ventured off-road to discover a world filled with stunning mountain ranges, vast plains, majestic lakes and pristine alpine environments. And the best thing about these breathtaking natural wonders? You can drive on them!

10. Evo 7 vs skateboard

Group N Mitsubishi Evo 7 rally car vs 16-year-old boy on a skateboard. Sounds a bit ridiculous, doesn't it? Surprisingly, it wasn't, since the skateboard was a modified all-terrain deck and was being ridden by a two-time world champion boarder. And while the board could leap over hills and generally avoid the track, the Evo had to stick to the road. Not surprisingly, the kid and board flew effortlessly across the finish line, while the Evo flew into a fence.

09. Running wild

One vehicle that had better luck against the skateboarder (primarily because it terrified him off the course) is the Bowler Wildcat. Unfortunately, though, when The Stig took it round the Top Gear track, the Wildcat could muster only 1 min 39s; placing it fourth last overall. The 300bhp, V8 engine wrapped in a giant roll-cage is much better suited to the rough and tumble of, say, a desert.

08. Carry On Caravanning

The humble caravan has suffered terribly at the hands of the Top Gear team. Dropped from cranes, crushed by limos and Volvos, crashed into bollards, used as a playing piece in darts and conkers games, and gutted by fire (once on a camping trip, once by the jet engine of a drag racer). You get the feeling they have something against the popular recreational off-roader. And you'd be right.

07. Ice-capades

Despite the ice being no thicker than a Weetabix, James and Jeremy faced off on a frozen Norwegian lake to prove James' theory that more power doesn't necessarily mean more speed. In a Land Rover Discovery, James completed the course in 2 mins 3s. In a Jaguar XK8, Jeremy failed to cross the finish line, but claimed victory anyway, arguing that he was more graceful. More graceful than what? A moose?

06. Jeep vs snowmobile

Using a vehicle to try to speed tunnel through dirt can get a bit ho-hum, so these Icelandic thrill-seekers have found a new, slightly trickier surface to drive on – water. Insane? Most probably. But, as Richard found out, not impossible. And with that conquest under their belt, they decided to try a snowmobile, which covered the half kilometre course on Lake Kleifarvatn quicker than the jeep.

05. Ice cream van

Speaking of idiotic jumping challenges, the team decided to, once and for all, answer an age-old question that has plagued man throughout the ages: can an ice cream van jump over four bouncing castles? And the answer? Er, no.

RRMMMBLL

FIREFORCE

04. Bravecart

Disregarding thousands of years of local knowledge, Jeremy set out to drive a Land Rover Discovery up a 1,007ft mountain near Cape Wrath in northern Scotland. All went according to plan, with the Disco adapting beautifully to the terrain. That was, of course, until it hit uneven ground. Fortunately, the locals emerged from behind a hill to winch the Disco out of trouble. Jeremy then completed the ascent by relying on a little of his own 'local knowledge' – he floored it.

03. Target practice

Range Rover is very proud of its super-charged V8 Sport. Boasting superior suspension and steering and a sporty spoiler at the front, it can out-manoeuvre, out-handle and out-run other vehicles in its class.

The British Army is similarly very proud of its V12 Challenger 2 tank. Like the Sport, it too boasts superior suspension and steering and can out-manoeuvre, out-handle and out-run other vehicles in its class. It doesn't, however, have a sporty spoiler.

What the Challenger 2 lacks in sporty front spoilers, it more than adequately makes up for with a 55 calibre L30A1 tank gun. Jeremy was certain the Sport could win against the Challenger 2. He was wrong.

02. Vroom, vroom... gurgle

Having failed dismally in their attempt to turn a Renault Espace people carrier into a convertible, the team's decision to convert three cars into amphibious vehicles was truly mind-boggling. After two days of toil, James' Triumph Herald sported a mast and sails, Richard's camper van became a houseboat and Jeremy's 'Toybota' Hilux, well, that basically just had a whopping great outboard motor strapped to its rear-end. Jeremy and Richard's efforts sank without experiencing much chop on the water. Only James managed to salvage any pride out of the exercise, living up to his nickname by captaining the slowest vessel ever launched.

01. Mini the Eagle

The 'Mini Cooper down a ski-jump' proved to be one of the team's finest moments – mainly because they had nothing to do with it.

Charged with the task of keeping the Mini in a straight line, James enlisted the help of some locals to fit skis to the wheels. Given the responsibility of powering the Mini, Jeremy made cups of tea, leaving the job to the United Kingdom Rocketry Association. As for Hammond, well, his barricade of loose snow and office furniture lacked basic functionality, due mainly to the fact it was on the wrong slope.

And when all was said, done and in position, the car failed to go anywhere near the target set by the human ski-jumper. But, as it turned out, none of that mattered.

Simply the opportunity to witness a Mini Cooper, powered by 1.5 tonnes of explosive thrust, screaming down a ski-jump into a barricade was brilliant enough to propel it into the first position on our list of Top 10 Off-roaders.

Get Across London

The new Mercedes GL... It is the **Chelsea-ist** of all the Chelsea tractors.

How closely were you paying attention when Top Gear's presenters raced each other across London at rush hour using a bike, a boat, a car and public transport?

Hidden in the square opposite are 20 London suburbs, landmarks and Tube stations. They were all either mentioned or seen on signs during the race. And for an extra challenge, find two extra town names: they're both places well outside London, but they're where Jeremy thinks James will end up!

Are we ready?
3... 2...

Hold on!
He's jumped the gun!

Go! Now!

VRROOMM

```
E K F N O T G N I S N E K O T T
O N B E O E G T U G D O B B N N
F A U T L S U T M M O A M A E G
A B A D R S N U G R T A N E M P
D L L T E S N B B T H F P T K I
O L B S T O E D E L T O R A N C
H I E T A T R R U F N O K D A C
A M R I W O S F A T P I R N B A
M R T E F E B T E R N O N B M D
M N H M A S U F I G N I L A E I
E R A U Q S R A G L A F A R T L
R T L I L A Y E E F M H W H T L
S K L S C T O A D R G C S E A Y
M L A T I R W A N D S W O R T H
I I T C G E E M O N U M E N T I
T O W E R B R I D G E H F K M S
H T V C H I S W I C K E R M G S
```

Kew	Albert Hall	King George V
Chiswick	Piccadilly	Tower Bridge
Ealing	Trafalgar Square	Huddersfield
Wandsworth	Embankment	Pontefract
Gunnersbury	Fulham	
Hammersmith	City Airport	
Battersea	Millbank	
Stamford Brook	Monument	
Kensington	Waterloo	

Did you go underground? Did it go dark? Flashing lights?

The Car – as an entity – lies **smashed** and **broken** in front of us... because of **you**. **He** beat you on **public transport.**

The Top Gear British Leyland Cars Challenge

The Top Gear production team say that British Leyland* was a miserable disaster and everything they ever made was rubbish. The chaps insist that some of the designs were quite clever and actually rather decent. Sounds like a challenge!

> Most **interesting** car they ever made. And most **radical**. And most **modern**.

> You've bought a piece of **cheese!**

The cars

Jeremy, Richard and James each bought a car with their own money. Completing the challenges set by the producers would win back some or all of their cash. Fill in the results table on the next page to work out if anyone came out ahead.

Richard: A Triumph Dolomite or 'Dolly'. The first car ever to have 16 valves, 4 per cylinder; the first British saloon car ever to have alloy wheels as standard; and the only car with wooden trim apparently made of unsanded floorboards.

£1,250

Jeremy: A Rover SD1. 3.5 litre V8 engine, 155bhp. Styled to look like a Ferrari Daytona... only with plum-coloured upholstery and non-working cruise control.

£1,100

James: An Austin Princess with hydrogas suspension (which has leaked on one side). The first car ever to obscure its wiper spindles under the bonnet. Wow.

£1,000

DAD 3521

* For younger readers, this was a huge British car manufacturer back in the days when cars were built by old blokes in overalls rather than robots.

Challenge 1: Reliability

The test: Drive 40 miles to receive the next challenge, without any mechanical problems. Easy.

The prize: £100 if they succeed.

The result: Only James could actually start his car. And Richard broke down again after 100 yards. Jeremy even managed to get his finger caught in a hole he found in his car.

FAIL

FAIL

FAIL

Oh **BEEP**. Gone the wrong way.

My **washing machine** moves around the **kitchen** faster than that!

Challenge 2: Power

The test: Beat the lap time of 1 min 11s set by The Stig in a Datsun 120Y at the top-secret MIRA test track (it's near Nuneaton, on the A5).

The prize: £10 for every second they beat The Stig by.

The result: Jeremy and Richard gave it all they could, but their cars were old and tired. Captain Slow managed to get lost. Jeremy and Richard got so bored waiting for him to finish they dropped the stopwatch.

Don't know (but not good)

1min 12sec

1min 16sec

RTP 837S

JHW 673X

SKREEEEEEEEEEEE

Challenge 3: Handbrake

The test: Drive up a one-in-three hill and stop. Put the car in neutral, apply the handbrake and get out of the car.

The prize: £100 if successful.

The result: James, remarkably, managed it without breaking a sweat. Jeremy produced an immense cloud of smoke that obscured his car, just trying to drive up the slope. Remarkably he claimed to have passed the test. Richard's Dolly proved sadly inadequate... again.

A good test of how **fast it goes backwards ... with** the **handbrake on.**

FAIL

With my sport suspension, I'm likely to become a human **omelette.**

Challenge 4: Egg

The test: Drive along MIRA's very bumpy cobbled road at 30mph with a colander of eggs fixed to the roof lining.

The prize: Each gram of egg left in the colander earns £10, but each bit of trim that falls off during the test will cost the chaps £10.

The result: James had the best suspension, but still ended up looking he had crashed into the back of a hen. Richard, on the other hand, got egg down his back (because he has to have his seat further forward) and lost rather a lot of his car. Jeremy only lost two bits of trim, but one of them was quite large. Door-sized, in fact.

4g of egg left, 2 trim pieces lost

0g of egg left, 6 trim pieces lost

4g of egg left, 2 trim pieces lost

HW 673X

KRUMP

Challenge 5: Water

The test: Drive around the Top Gear track as far as possible... while wearing a drysuit... with the car full of water. This tests both build quality (how well the panels fit together) and performance (how fast it can go full of a ton of water). When the water level drops below the bottom of the steering wheel, stop.

The prize: 20p for every yard covered.

The result: Fire trucks provided the water, the doors were sealed with gaffer tape and air was delivered through a snorkel. Richard managed a respectable half-lap. James looked dodgy to start, but managed to lap Richard. Jeremy's Rover couldn't even be filled with two truckloads of water and three hoses, so he set off when everyone got bored. Almost immediately, another door fell off!

4,500 yards

10 yards

> You've been **lapped** by Captain Slow!

> Doesn't happen every day. In an **Austin Princess** full of **water.**

1,500 yards

SPALOOSSHH

The scores

Fill in everyone's scores from each round. Can you work out if anyone got their money back?

	Cost of car	Reliability	Power	Handbrake	Egg	Water	**TOTAL**
RICHARD Dolly							
JEREMY Rover							
JAMES Princess							

> British Leyland **DID** make a good car. And **here** it is: a beige Austin Princess with a **brown** vinyl roof!

Power Words

If it's every boy's dream to drive a high-performance supercar, then it must be every high-performance supercar's dream to be put through its paces on the Top Gear test track. That's where The Stig pushes cars beyond their capabilities.

Some say he doesn't have a favourite, but if you complete the puzzle below you'll reveal the name of one street-legal production monster that would come close to holding a special place in The Stig's heart – if he had one.

01 With the power to turn Jeremy's face into Play-doh, this skeleton of a supercar is, like its name, super small.

02 This manufacturer created possibly the most powerful convertible ever with its Biturbo Roadster.

03 German powerhouse, manufacturer of the 10th fastest power lapper.

04 Songwriter popular with old people, and a bend on the Top Gear test track.

05 The Evo 8 is the four-door firebrand of this Japanese car maker.

06 A Ferrari 'Enzo in drag' it may be, but the MC12 is all _ _ _ _ _ _ _ _ _ _ _.

07 Proudly British, this Leicester-born beast is faster than a Porsche 911.

08 A F1 heavyweight and one of the quickest ways to get to Oslo.

09 A corner on the Top Gear test track and an American city.

10 James Bond's latest ride.

Answers

Page 9 1: A snowmobile. 2: Koenigsegg CCX. 3: Language tapes, romantic novels, self-help tapes. 4: Sweden. 5: 1 min, 17.3 sec

Page 14 1: Chevrolet Lacetti. 2: Dampervan. 3: Sweden. 4: Mini 5: Silverstone. 6: White. 7: Toyota. 8: Gambon. 9: Daniel. 10: Bull. 11: Bugatti Veyron. 12: Oliver. 13: Pagani. Hidden star: **Lewis Hamilton.**

Page 15

Page 18

```
O E U S A I O O O U D N M R G T A N
X A P R V C A U D R A T E R C D N E
O E T E B A T O T C P M Y P L A I D
A O E V S V A P D S O T I I B A A O
E G A T N A V N I T R A M N O T S A
A G S C D K A X H Y S A A I A N T D
L O A A T A T C S A C O A X K I O N
G O N M O A O C S S H T A G U I N O
F Y T F N Z R G A A E H E D E G M Z
A A M U O R N G B I C C N S S A A I
O I T R S R F E X A A E I G E X R N
O F A J N E D S I E Y R T G T G T A
A X S E N O X G A R M O M N N E I G
S N O R Y E V I T E G U B M E N A
A T N E T N N N G T N R A C C R D H
A M N I N N E E S E A T R T R G B H
E N E R S F O O G N M X C E H Z S G
J A G U A R X K R N R I A H F T N X
```

Page 19 1: Porsche. 2: Lamborghini. 3: Ferrari. 4: Volkswagen. 5: Lotus. 6: Aston Martin. 7: Maserati.

Page 26 1: Porsche Carrera. 2: Lamborghini Murcielago. 3: Ariel Atom. 4: Pagani Zonda F. 5: Bowler Wildcat. 6: Maserati Bora. 7: Ford Anglia. 8: Nissan Micra. 9: Renault Espace. 10: Range Rover.

Page 27 The highlighted letters can be rearranged to spell **Koenigsegg.**

1	T	O	Y	O	T	A					
2		B	U	G	A	T	T	I			
3			S	I	L	V	E	R	S	T	O	N	E
4	P	O	R	S	C	H	E				
5	I	C	E	H	O	C	K	E	Y		
6		H	A	M	I	L	T	O	N		
7	F	O	R	D	G	T					
8		H	A	M	S	T	E	R			
9	L	A	M	B	O	R	G	H	I	N	I
10	L	E	Y	L	A	N	D				

Page 32 1: True. 2: True. 3: False: He owns a cat named Fusker. 4: False: It was Paddington Bear toys. 5: True. 6: True. It was in 2005. 7: False. 8: False. 9: True. 10: False.

Page 33 James gets nearest.

Page 42

```
S E M X N V H Z U N E O G O H T L I S
A O Q M Y T G F N E J N T E Y O H L T
U S A E R R M S E N I I J E L R I T H
C P I Z I I L E C D F K D F A O I T I
R I R W I G D S D P O L C I O L A G F
Y N S C M Q O I G Z E R O A P L E N E
D N X Q E N K N P M T F F T E S D I Y
G I T O H S I O L L A W E R I T E R X
D N N O Y K U N D E R S T E E R H E F
T G I O A I P P O W E R F U L S N N T
X G B R M F E H E S L E E W C R L R O
S Y B N E I A L H R E E P C E O M O L
E R B I F N O B R A T X E O M N C O
G C L I D S R R C R C H T E D V K E T
M L Z L T O P O O A A S A T E E L T A
C N I I B J M F C P R H E R P L M I P
C N T X G X N R S E T L O S G A H T H
G E E P O W A S V G N I H C E E R C S
M W C B O S N O I T C U R T S E D F W
H O W D H I G H N P B L X F E G I S C
```

Page 43

Page 48 1: b, Bacharach. 2: c, Mercedes McLaren SLR. 3: c, Silver. 4: b, A truffle. 5: c, VW Golf. 6: a, Rinspeed Splash. 7: c, Six. 8: b, Jeremy. 9: b, Oliver. 10: a, Aston Martin DB9. 11: b, France. 12: b, he's got a big beer gut. 13: b, £65 million. 14: a, The company's founder. 15: b, VW Beetle. 16: c, Jeremy. 17: b, Jennifer Saunders. 18: a, Caravan Club Towing Car of the Year. 19: c, Messerschmitt. 20: a, Nissan Micra.

Page 52 James doesn't make it to the finish.

Page 53 The correct order is E, I, B, H, G, A, D, F, C.

Page 60 The route reads I KNOW EXACTLY WHERE I AM GOING

Page 61 A-5, B-6, C-4, D-3, E-2, F-1.

Page 67

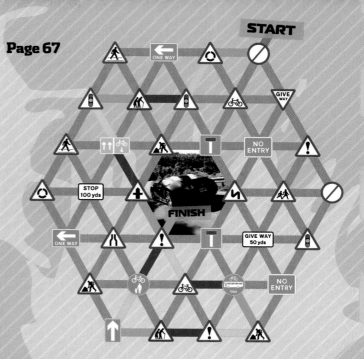

Page 85

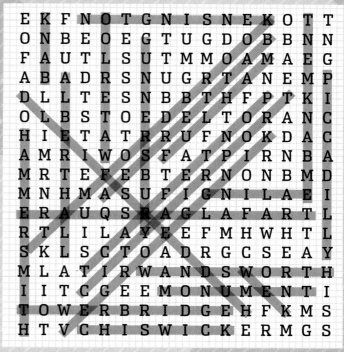

Page 89 Richard earned £240, Jeremy earned £122 and James earned an impressive £1020 – covering the cost of his car.

Page 90

1. ATOM
2. BRABUS
3. MERCEDES
4. BACHARACH
5. MITSUBISHI
6. MASERATI
7. NOBLE
8. FERARRI
9. CHICAGO
10. ASTONMARTIN